MR. WILSON'S CABINET
of WONDER

Also by Lawrence Weschler

A Miracle, a Universe:
Settling Accounts with Torturers

Shapinsky's Karma, Boggs's Bills
and Other True-Life Tales

David Hockney's Cameraworks

The Passion of Poland

Seeing Is Forgetting the Name of the Thing One Sees:
A Life of Contemporary Artist Robert Irwin

Charles Willson Peale,
The Artist in His Museum
(1822)

MR. WILSON'S
CABINET
of
WONDER

Lawrence Weschler

PANTHEON BOOKS   NEW YORK

All rights reserved under International and
Pan-American Copyright Conventions. Published in
the United States by Pantheon Books, a division of
Random House, Inc., New York, and simultaneously in
Canada by Random House of Canada Limited, Toronto.

Portions of this book were previously published, in an
abridged form, in *Harper's.*

*Grateful acknowledgment is made to the following for
permission to reprint previously published material:* · *RES:*
Excerpts from "Inquiry as Collection" by Adalgisa
Lugli (*RES,* Autumn 1986). Reprinted by permission of
RES. · *Jay's Journal of Anomalies:* Excerpt from an
article by Ricky Jay *(Jay's Journal of Anomalies,* vol. 1,
no. 1, spring 1994). Reprinted by permission of *Jay's
Journal of Anomalies,* published by W&V Dailey,
8216 Melrose Avenue, Los Angeles, CA 90046.

Library of Congress Cataloging-in-Publication Data

Weschler, Lawrence.
Mr. Wilson's cabinet of wonder / Lawrence
Weschler.
p.   cm.
ISBN 0-679-43998-6
1. Museum of Jurassic Technology–History.
2. Wilson, David.   3. Popular culture–United
States–History.   4. Museum–Philosophy.
5. Collectors and collecting–History. I. Title.
AM101.L725W47   1995
069´5–dc20   95-5996

Book design by M. Kristen Bearse

Manufactured in the United States of America

4 6 8 9 7 5 3

———————————— ❧❧❧ ————————————

For Sara
my own living wonder

—— ❧ ❧ ❧ ——

Nothing is too wonderful to be true.
—MICHAEL FARADAY

Contents

PART I

Inhaling the Spore

Megaloponera foetens *(the Cameroonian stink ant) with forehead rampant*

Deep in the Cameroonian rain forests of west-central Africa there lives a floor-dwelling ant known as *Megaloponera foetens*, or more commonly, the stink ant. This large ant—indeed, one of the very few capable of emitting a cry audible to the human ear—survives by foraging for food among the fallen leaves and undergrowth of the extraordinarily rich rain-forest floor.

On occasion, while thus foraging, one of these ants will become infected by inhaling the microscopic spore of a fungus from the genus *Tomentella*, millions of which rain down upon the forest floor from somewhere in the canopy above. Upon being inhaled, the spore lodges itself inside the ant's tiny brain and immediately begins to grow, quickly fomenting bizarre behavioral changes in its ant host. The creature appears troubled and confused, and presently, for the first time in its life, it leaves the forest floor and begins an arduous climb up the stalks of vines and ferns.

Driven on and on by the still-growing fungus, the ant finally achieves a seemingly prescribed height whereupon, utterly spent, it impales the plant with its mandibles and, thus affixed, waits to die. Ants that have met their doom in this fashion are quite a common sight in certain sections of the rain forest.

The fungus, for its part, lives on: it continues to consume the brain, moving on through the rest of the nervous system and, eventually, through all the soft tissue that remains of the ant. After approximately two weeks, a spikelike protrusion erupts from out of what had once been the ant's head. Growing to a length of about an inch and a half, the spike features a bright orange tip, heavy-laden with spores, which now begin to rain down onto the forest floor for other unsuspecting ants to inhale.

THE GREAT MIDCENTURY American neurophysiologist Geoffrey Sonnabend inhaled his spore, as it were, one in-

Madalena Delani and Geoffrey Sonnabend at Iguazú Falls (1936)

somniac night in 1936 while convalescing from a combined physical and nervous breakdown (brought on, in part, by the collapse of his earlier investigation into memory pathways in carp) at a small resort near the majestic Iguazú Falls, in the so-called Mesopotamian region along the Argentinean-Brazilian-Paraguayan frontier. Earlier that evening, he had attended a recital of German Romantic lieder given by the great Romanian-American vocalist, Madalena Delani. Delani, one of the leading soloists on the international concert circuit of her day, had won frequent praise from the likes of the *New York Times*'s Sidney Soledon, who once surmised that the uniquely plaintive quality of her vocal instrument—its texture, as he described it, of being "steeped in a sense of loss"—might have derived from the fact that the singer suffered from a form of Korsakov's syndrome, with its attendant obliteration of virtually all short- and intermediate-term memory, with the exception, in her case, of the memory of music itself.

Although Geoffrey left the concert hall that evening without ever meeting Delani, the concert had electrified him, and through a sleepless night he conceived, as if in a single blast of inspiration, the entire model of intersecting plane and cone that was to constitute the basis for his radical new theory of memory, a theory he'd spend the next decade painstakingly elaborating in his three-volume *Obliscence: Theories of Forgetting and the Problem of Matter* (Chicago: Northwestern University Press, 1946). Memory, for Sonnabend, was an illusion. Forgetting, not remembering, was the inevitable outcome of all experience. From this perspective, as he explained in the introduction to his turgid masterwork, "We, amnesiacs all, condemned to live in an eternally fleeting present, have created the most elaborate of human constructions, memory, to buffer ourselves against the intolerable knowledge of the irreversible passage of time and irre-trievability of its moments and events" (p. 16). He him-self went on to expand on this doctrine through the explication of an increasingly intricate model in which a so-called Cone of Obliscence is bisected by Planes of Ex-perience, which are continually slicing through the cone at changing though precise angles. The theory was per-haps at its most suggestive as it broached such uncanny shadow phenomena as the experiences of premonition, déjà vu, and foreboding. But once the plane of any par-ticular experience had passed through the cone, the ex-perience was irretrievably forgotten—and all else was illusion. A particularly haunting conclusion, in that no sooner had Sonnabend published his magnum opus than both he and it fell largely into oblivion.

As for Delani, ironically, utterly unbeknownst to Sonnabend, she herself had perished in a freak automo-bile accident within a few days of her concert at Iguazú Falls.

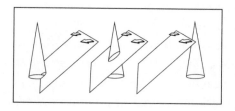

Plane of Experience bisecting Cone of Obliscence

*Dozo dwelling pierced
by* deprong mori

FOR HIS PART, Donald R. Griffith, Rockefeller University's eminent chiroptologist (and author of *Listening in the Dark: Echolocation in Bats and Men*), appears to have inhaled something suspiciously sporelike back in 1952, while reading the field reports of an obscure late-nineteenth-century American ethnographer named Bernard Maston. While doing field work, in 1872, among the Dozo of the Tripsicum Plateau of the circum-Caribbean region of northern South America, Maston reported having heard several accounts of the *deprong mori*, or piercing devil, which he described as "a small demon which the local savages believe able to penetrate solid objects," such as the walls of their thatch huts and, in one instance, even a child's outstretched arm.

Almost eighty years later, while reviewing some of Maston's notes in the Archive, Donald R. Griffith, for some reason, as he later recounted, "smelled a bat." He and a band of assistants undertook an arduous eight-month expedition to the Tripsicum Plateau, where Griffith grew increasingly convinced that he was dealing not with just any bat but with a very special bat indeed: specifically, the tiny *Myotis lucifugus*, which though previously documented had never before been studied in detail. It became Griffith's hypothesis that while most bats deploy frequencies in the ultrasonic range to assist them in

Echolocation in bats

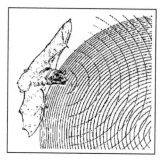

the echolocation that enables them to fly in the dark, *Myotis lucifugus* had evolved a highly specialized form of echolocation based upon ultraviolet wavelengths, which even, in some instances, verged into the neighboring X-ray band of the wave spectrum. Furthermore, these particular bats had evolved highly elaborate nose leaves, or horns, which allowed them to focus their echo-wave transmissions in a narrow beam. All of which would account for the wide range of bizarre effects described by Maston's informants.

Griffith and his team lacked only proof. Time after time, the little devils, on the very verge of capture, would fly seamlessly through their nets. So Griffith devised a brilliant snaring device, consisting of five solid-lead walls, each one eight inches thick, twenty feet high, and two hundred feet long—all of them arrayed in a radial pattern, like spokes of a giant wheel, along the forest

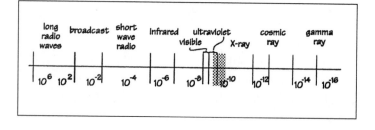

Electromagnetic spectrum

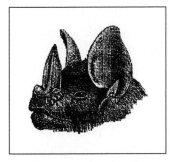

Elaborate nose leaves

floor. The team affixed seismic sensors all along the walls in an intricate grid-like pattern, and proceeded to wait.

For two months, the monitors recorded not a thing—surely the bats were simply avoiding the massive, and massively incongruous, lead walls—and Griffith began to despair of ever confirming his hypothesis. Finally, however, early on the morning of August 18th at 4:13 A.M., the sensors recorded a pock. The number-three wall had received an impact of magnitude 10×3 ergs twelve feet above the forest floor and 193 feet out from the center of the wheel. The team members carted an X-ray viewing device out to the indicated spot, and sure enough, at a depth of $7\frac{1}{8}$ inches, they located the first *Myotis lucifugus* ever contained by man, "eternally frozen in a mass of solid lead."

Megaloponera foetens, *Myotis lucifugus*, Geoffrey Sonnabend and Madalena Delani, the Dozo and the *deprong mori*, Bernard Maston

Myotis lucifugus, *"eternally frozen in a mass of solid lead"*

and Donald R. Griffith—these and countless other spores rain down and down upon a small nondescript storefront operation located along the main commercial drag of downtown Culver City in the middle of West Los Angeles's endless pseudo-urban sprawl: the Museum of Jurassic Technology, according to a fading blue banner facing the street.

Flanked on one side by a carpet store and a derelict (seemingly long-abandoned) real estate office, and on the other by a forensics lab and a Thai restaurant (and on the first side, a bit further along, by a PIP printing outlet, an India Sweets and Spices mart, and a Hare Krishna

temple; while on the other, further on up the block, by Manuel's Auto Body Shop, In-and-Out Burger, and a Blockbuster Video franchise), the museum presents precisely the sort of anonymous-looking facade one might easily pass right by. Which most days would be just as well, since most days it's closed.

But if you'd happened to have heard of it, as I began hearing of it a couple of years ago on my occasional visits to L.A. (it's been at its present site for a bit over seven years now) and thus actively sought it out; or else, if you just happened to be dallying at the bus stop right outside its portals on one of those occasions when it actually was

The 9300 block of Venice Boulevard, Culver City, California;
at center, the Museum of Jurassic Technology

open (Thursday evenings, and Saturdays and Sundays noon to six)—and bus waits in L.A. tend to be endless at *all* times—well, then, your curiosity piqued, you might just find yourself going up and tentatively pressing its door buzzer. While waiting for an answer, you might study, for example, the curious little diorama slotted into the wall off to the side of the entry (a diminutive white urn surrounded by floating pearlescent moths) or another equally perplexing diorama off to the other side of the entry (three chemistry-set bottles arrayed in a curiously loving display: oxide of titanium, oxide of iron, and alumina, according to their labels); or, still waiting, your gaze might float up to another banner rippling above the entryway (this one featuring the image of a strangely generic archaic sculpted head—part Minoan, part Easter Island—with, above it, the letters A, E, and N, each capped by a long macron) . . .

At length the door is likely to open, and usually it will be David Hildebrand Wilson himself, the museum's founder and director, a small and unassuming man, perhaps in his mid-forties, who will be smiling there solicitously (as if it were specifically you he'd been expecting all along) and happily bidding you to enter.

It's dark in there. As your eyes adjust, you take in an old wooden desk, on top of which a small sign proposes an admissions donation of $2.50, though Wilson quickly assures you that this is a neighborhood museum and hence free to anybody from the neighborhood, and that, furthermore, he considers the bus-stop bench to be an integral part of the neighborhood. He leaves it to you to decide what that means, and for that matter, he leaves it all to you. He has returned to his seat behind the desk and to his reading (two dusty, antiquated books, the last time I was there, one entitled *Mental Hospitals*, the other *The Elements of Folk Psychology*). The foyer, as it were, features a kind of half-hearted attempt at a gift shop, but probably you won't tarry long as your curiosity is already being drawn toward the museum proper.

And it's here that you'll encounter, across a maze of discrete alcoves, in meticulous displays exactingly laid out, the ant, the bat, the falls, the diva, the insomniac . . . A preserved sample of the stink ant, for example, has its mandibles embedded into the stalk of a plastic fern in a standard natural-history-museum-style diorama. Sure enough, a thin spike is erupting out of its head. There's a telephone receiver beside the vitrine, and if you pick it up you'll hear the entire history of *Megaloponera foetens*, largely as I conveyed it at the outset of this account.

A whole wing of the museum has been given over to the so-called Sonnabend-Delani Halls, where, among other things, you'll find an astonishingly well-realized aquarium-sized diorama of Iguazú Falls, complete with gushing, recirculating water. It turns out, or so the nearby phone receiver informs you, that the Falls were doubly significant in Sonnabend's life, for they were also the place where, fifty years earlier, his parents had first met. His father, Wilhelm, a young German structural engineer, had been trying to span the Falls with a vast suspension bridge, but the project came to naught, his dream collapsing irrevocably into the abyss a mere day short of completion. From either side of the diorama at the museum, you can see where Wilhelm's bridge would have gone: from head on, you can peer through an eyepiece and, miraculously, see the bridge itself, hovering serenely over the cataract. The effect is so vividly realized that you'll look again from the sides—your eyes, or something, must be playing tricks on you—but nothing is there except falling water.

Sonnabend's actual desk and study have been salvaged and painstakingly re-created. There's a wall of photos detailing the stages of his life and his parents' lives and a whole documentary embolism, as it were, devoted to the career of one Charles Gunther, an eccentric Chicago millionaire confectioner, who happened to be visiting Iguazú at the time of Wilhelm's debacle and who became the young engineer's patron in the years thereafter, bringing him back with him to Chicago and securing him employment as director of the reconstruction of the Chicago bridge system in the wake of that city's Great Fire. Gunther himself, it appears, was quite a character in his own right, an inveterate collector of historical arcana and natural curiosa who even had an entire Confederate prison—the Libby, in Richmond, Virginia—dismantled, brick by brick, and reassembled in Chicago, so as to house his prodigious hoard, which included the very tables upon which the Emancipation Proclamation and the Appomattox Surrender were signed, as well as a swath of dried skin sloughed off by the serpent who first seduced Woman in the Garden of Eden—all properly certified with the requisite letters of authentication—a bounteous trove which, upon his death, came to constitute a cornerstone of the Chicago Historical Society, under whose auspices large portions

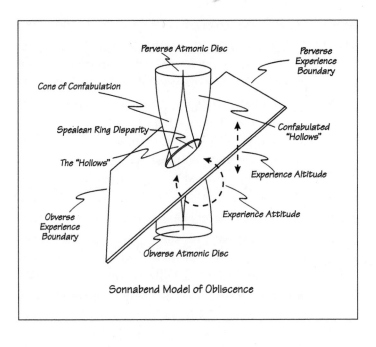

Perverse Atmonic Disc

Perverse Experience Boundary

Cone of Confabulation

Spealean Ring Disparity

Confabulated "Hollows"

The "Hollows"

Experience Altitude

Obverse Experience Boundary

Experience Attitude

Obverse Atmonic Disc

Sonnabend Model of Obliscence

The Sonnabend Model of Obliscence

of it can be seen to this day. Or, anyway, so the sequence of phone receivers at the museum allege as they guide you through the tale.

You can sit on a bench, pick up another receiver, and have Sonnabend's whole theory laid out for you through a series of haunting, sequentially lit dioramas of variously intersecting (and compoundingly complexifying) cones and planes, complete with a representation of such technical subtleties as the perverse and obverse experience boundaries, the Spelean Ring Disparity, the Hollows, and, perhaps most provocatively, the Cone of Confabulation. (The voice in the receiver, the same voice as in all the other receivers, it may occur to you, is in fact the same bland, slightly unctuous voice you've heard in every museum slide show or Acoustiguide tour or PBS nature special you've ever endured: the reassuringly measured voice of unassailable institutional authority.)

Over to the side there's a whole dark room devoted exclusively to Madalena Delani. By entering it you trigger an elaborate *son et lumière* presentation, back-lit slides along the walls rising up and fading in time with the narration. In the middle of the room, a glass-case table offers up jewelry, a feathered boa, musical scores, and other memorabilia; at the back of the room, a headless mannequin, swathed in one of the diva's last dresses, oversees the séance. As you leave these halls, you may notice a tangent exhibit that evokes the contrasting memory theories of a turn-of-the-century French novelist named Marcel Proust: the vitrine contains a plate of madeleines, a single bite having been taken out of one of them ("Madeleines, madeleines," you may find your mind thrumming, "Madalena Delani . . .").

Around the corner you come upon another bench and another phone receiver and another elaborate display, this one detailing the bizarrely intersecting careers of Maston and Griffith. Once again, narrow-beam spotlights rise up and fade away, guiding you through the narrative—including a detailed exposition of how echolocation works in bats, complete with charts and graphs—culminating with a view of a solid tranche from the lead wall itself, one which presently becomes illumined, as if from within, so that you can actually see the bat embedded there, arrested in midflight.

Through much of these explorations, you may well be the only person inside the museum, aside from Wilson, and he's a bit of a piercing devil himself. He pads about silently as you lose yourself in the various exhibits. One moment he's at his desk; the next he's gone, though who knows where?—perhaps to a workroom secreted at the rear of the store; a few moments later, however, he's back reading at his desk, as if he was never gone at all. You

continue to poke about—there are a good dozen other exhibits up at any given time—and presently, eerily, you become aware of strains of Bach being played on . . . on . . . could it be an accordion? The desk chair is empty, the front door has been left slightly ajar: Wilson is on the sidewalk, blithely serenading the passing traffic.

You leave him to it. You

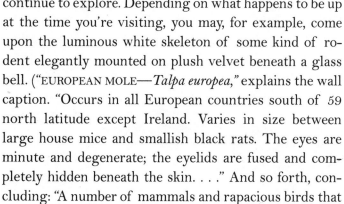

continue to explore. Depending on what happens to be up at the time you're visiting, you may, for example, come upon the luminous white skeleton of some kind of rodent elegantly mounted on plush velvet beneath a glass bell. ("EUROPEAN MOLE—*Talpa europea,*" explains the wall caption. "Occurs in all European countries south of 59 north latitude except Ireland. Varies in size between large house mice and smallish black rats. The eyes are minute and degenerate; the eyelids are fused and completely hidden beneath the skin. . . ." And so forth, concluding: "A number of mammals and rapacious birds that are not offended by the mole's musky odor prey upon them.") In another glass case you can study "The Rose Collection of Now-Extinct Nineteenth-Century French Moths." ("There's a slight misnomer there," Wilson informed me solicitously the first time I peered into that case. He happened to be passing silently by. "Most of those particular moths are indeed French, but a few are actually Flemish—although with some it's hard to tell.")

A spotlight shines down on an otherwise darkened wall, highlighting a complicated and almost indecipherable map. The nearby caption is headlined, "THE SIEGE AND BATTLE OF PAVIA, Fig. 74, Cat. no. 263" and goes on to ventilate, in bewildering detail, the conflicting estimations of several long-dead chroniclers, none of whom, clearly, was ever there—wherever *there* is or was (this minor detail, for some reason, has been occluded).

"We see the subtlest forces, obeying the most capricious behests of the human mind," declares another wall caption—otherwise untethered—citing as its source simply: "Buckle (3): 03." Inside one vitrine there's a scrupulously wrought scale model of Noah's Ark, with a cutaway revealing the stalls below deck. "1 inch = 12.5 cubits," advises the caption. The model itself, propped up upon two silently pumping pistons, bobs languorously.

Along a nearby wall (just off to the side, actually, from the vitrine containing the spike-

The Ark (scale,
1 inch: 12.5 cubits)

sprouting ant), there's a pretty standard natural-history-museum-style array of mounted horns and antlers—standard, that is, with the exception of one, the smallest of the lot: a solitary hairy protrusion. (A nearby caption cites the testimony, inside quotation marks, of an "Early visitor to the *Musaeum Tradescantianum,* The Ark" to the effect that "We were shown an extraordinarily curious horn which had grown on the back of a woman's head. . . . It is somewhat of a curiosity [for] it appears that men-folk bear their horns in front and such women theirs behind. It was noted on a label that it originated from a Mary Davis of Saughall in Cheshire *an aet 71 an. Dn. 1688.* No doubt it will have been mentioned in the *Transactiones Angl.,* or in the *Hist. nat.* of Cheshire. The horn was blackish in color, not very thick or hard, but well proportioned." As, indeed, this specimen is.)

The Antler Wall at the MJT

The horn of Mary Davis of Saughall

Another display, entitled "Protective Auditory Mimicry" allows you to compare, by pushing the requisite buttons, the sounds made by certain small, iridescent beetles, when threatened, with those made by certain similarly sized and hued pebbles "while at rest." Another glass case contains, according to its caption, a "Zinc-inlaid black onyx box used for holding sacrificial human hearts. For as yet unknown reasons, the remains of dried sacrificial blood appear phosphorescent when viewed through polarizing material like that at the front of the case." At the front of the case, a ponderous viewing apparatus hovers expectantly atop an empty display stand. "Specimen Temporarily Removed for Study," a small sign apologizes.

There is an entire closet-sized alcove given over to a special exhibition entitled "No One May Ever Have the Same Knowledge Again: Letters to the Mount Wilson Observatory, 1915–1935," wherein are lovingly displayed twenty-two framed holograph communiqués from a purported file of forty-three such missives originally received by the astronomers at the famous observatory, located in the mountains above Pasadena, California. An introductory caption to the entire exhibit explains how "Letters of this kind began arriving at the Observatory as early as 1911 [the institution was founded in 1905] and continue to arrive even today." The astronomers dutifully filed them away. "The information contained in this class of letter," the legend goes on, "was typically of astronomical or cosmological concern. These individuals had gleaned the information they wished to communicate either by experimentation, observation, or intuition and invariably felt a strong sense of urgency in their need to communicate their observations to the observers at Mount Wilson."

Such was certainly the case with one Mrs. Alice May Williams, of Auckland, New Zealand, lines from one of whose letters provide this exhibit with its title: "I am not after money & I am not a fraud," she assures the astronomers, going on to explain how

> I believe I have some knowledge which you gentlemen should have. If I die my knowledge may die with me, & no one may ever have the same knowledge again. Because if people hear talking they want stick, they go & do away with their selves. I have gone through frightful things still I go through it & I am beginning to get knowledge.

That letter is presently followed by several others in which Mrs. Williams goes on to lay out her various discoveries regarding the types of beings living on other planets, their flight machines, their intentions and capabilities ("I believe the people of the other world have glasses they can see you with. They can draw you to them"). And in so doing, as the other yellowing pages in the exhibit make clear, she is joining an entire world community of like-visited visionaries.

May Wiltse, of Venice, California, for instance, writes the observatory's founder, Dr. George Hale, how "In 1916 I went to Washington, D.C., and transmuted silver into gold for the United States government and I have their reports. BUT IT WAS HUSHED up for reasons I cannot explain." A few pages later she goes on to quote from a letter she'd managed to elicit from another scientist she'd apparently been hounding for some time to the effect that "I am glad to know you long ago discovered ALL the wonderful things modern science is daily discovering." She reiterates the phrase—" 'ALL the secrets of nature,' not one BUT ALL"—and modestly accepts the characterization. Bobbie Merlino of Atlantic City, New Jersey, in a note dated December 4, 1932, offers his (her?) services for an eventual flight to Mars: "I readily understand that is a very dangerous expedition that we may never return but as long as I just take one glimpse at it I am satisfy if I die on the Planet I've always planned to visit. I am not out of my mind. I am as sane as anyone and I am very serious about this matter. . . ." In 1920 an unknown person who simply signed his meticulously calligraphed note "Historian, Boston, Mass." offered an elaborate proof to the effect that "THE EARTH is FLAT and STANDS FAST." John Rounds of Boscobel, Wisconsin, a few years later offered an even more convoluted—indeed, positively loopy—proof that "the Earth is *not* flat" and that, in fact, "it turns around the sun," as if he were the first person ever to have hazarded such a daring hypothesis. The passion emanating from such pages seems authentically heartfelt, and the pages themselves, appropriately aged, seem like they must be genuine.

Just a few feet away from the alcove containing the Mount Wilson letters exhibit, there's another aquarium-sized vitrine containing another large piece of serious-looking scientific apparatus, this one hovering above a black turntable along which are evenly spaced five small concave glass dishes, each harboring a tiny mound of powder. The five dishes are labeled "POSSESSION," "DELUSION," "PARANOIA," "SCHIZOPHRENIA," and "REASON." There is no other caption. But on closer examination, it appears some kind of mishap must recently have occurred: the heavily barreled measuring apparatus has descended too far into the dish labeled "REASON" and the dish has shattered, spilling shards and powder onto the turntable. "Out of order," advises a tiny sign taped to the face of the glass case.

By this time, you too may be starting to feel a bit out of order, all shards and powder. You head back to the foyer, where Wilson is again ensconced behind his desk, absorbed in his reading, the accordion resting along the wall by his side like a snoozing pet. You putter among the giftware, confused, hesitant. You poke among the monographs: perhaps they can help. Three little booklets are in fact being offered for sale, exemplars from an apparent series entitled "Contributions from the Museum of Jurassic Technology," which in turn appear to have been excerpted—or so the title apparatus on their covers would lead one to believe—from a multivolume *Supplement to a Chain of Flowers.* The monograph on Geoffrey Sonnabend is thus *An Encapsulation by Valentine Worth,* excerpted from "Volume V, no. 5 (First edition, abridged)" of the *Supplement to a Chain* (its text closely parallels the museum's own slide presentation, or maybe it's vice versa). The monograph on Maston, Griffith, and the *deprong mori* is actually a "Second edition, revised" from "Volume IV, no. 7." And then, as well, there's a curious monograph *On the Foundations of the Museum: The Thums, Gardeners and Botanists* (Third edition, revised) with a text attributed to Illera Edoh, Keeper of the Foundations Collections, whose magisterial account is liberally festooned with maniacally niggling footnotes, along such lines as: "Bird, 132, vol. 4, 337. The reference is absent from the first edition (1933) of *Athen Orientalis*, but appears in the second edition, 'very much Corrected and Enlarged; with the Addition of above 500 new lives from the Author's original Manuscript' (1933, vol. 2, col. 888) . . . although Bird's testimony would seem to be of very dubious value."

Each of the monographs is described, on its copyright page, as having been "Published in the United States by the Society for the Diffusion of Useful Information . . . in cooperation with the Visitors to the Museum by the Delegates of the Press." The press in question is, of course, the Society for the Diffusion of Useful Information Press, and its address is given as "9091 Divide Place, West Covina, California OX2 6DP" (bizarre zip!), though it appears to have other outposts as well, and they in turn are fastidiously laid out:

Billings   Bogata   Bhopal   Beirut
Bowling Green   Buenos Aires   Campton
Dayton   Dar es Salaam   Düsseldorf
Fort Wayne   Indianapolis   Lincoln
Mar en Beg   Mar en Mor
Nannin   Pretoria   Teheran
Socorro   Terra Haute   Ulster

So, obviously the monographs will not have helped at all, and by now you are completely at sea. "Um, excuse me," you may at length hazard, approaching Wilson at his desk. "Um, what exactly *is* this place?"

"Excuse me," I asked at just such a moment somewhere toward the end of my first visit. "Um, what kind of place *is* this exactly?" Wilson looked up from his reading: beatific deadpan.

I suppose I should say something here about Wilson's own presence, his own look, for it is of a piece with his museum. I have described him as diminutive, though a better word might be *simian*. His features are soft and yet precise, a broad forehead, short black hair graying at the sides, a close-cropped version of an Amish beard fringing his face and filling into his cheeks (though with no mustache, and the space between the bottom of his nose and upper lip is notably broad). He wears circular glasses which somehow accentuate the elfin effect. He's been described as Ahab inhabiting the body of Puck (a pixie Ahab, a monomaniacal Puck), but the best description I ever heard came from his wife, Diana (no particular giant herself—their friends sometimes refer to the two of them together as "the little Wilsons"), who one day characterized his looks for me as *neanderthal*. "I'm serious," she laughed. "There's all this physical evidence." (As a doctoral candidate in anthropology at UCLA, she ought to know.) "His browridge, for instance. With the rest of us it's smooth, but his definitely juts out. He has a little bun at the back of his skull—it's not flat like the rest of ours. The Neanderthals had enormous jaws, and David's dentist once told him in amazement that there was room enough for a whole extra set of molars at the back of his. If you look closely at his arms and legs, the lower bones seem proportionally longer and the upper ones shorter than with the rest of us—exactly as with them. Once we were at the Field Museum in Chicago, looking at a display about cavemen, and noticing all these similarities, we were almost rolling in the aisles. Everything the same, except, of course, that they were heavier, and he's light—so that, actually, he's more like a *pubescent* Neanderthal. He has this ridge, too, running down the middle of the top of his skull. That's *pre*-Neanderthal, actually—it served as a kind of attachment for those big jaw muscles. I mentioned that once to one of my professors and he said, 'Oh yeah, Eskimos have those too.' But I mean—'My husband is *not* an Eskimo,' I had to remind him."

"Well," Wilson replied coolly that first afternoon, un-fazed, from behind his wooden desk (obviously he gets asked this sort of question all the time). "As you can see, we're a small natural history museum with an emphasis on curiosities and technological innovation." He paused, and then went on: "We're definitely interested in pre-senting phenomena that other natural history museums seem unwilling to present." He could apparently sense that I was still a bit bewildered. "The name lends a sense of what's inside but doesn't refer to a specific geologic time," he offered, helpfully. He then reached into his drawer and pulled out a pamphlet. "Here, this might be useful."

The image on the pamphlet's cover was of the same archaic head as on the banner outside. "THE MUSEUM OF JURASSIC TECHNOLOGY—AND YOU," the headline around the head announced portentously. Inside, the pamphlet opened with a General Statement:

> The Museum of Jurassic Technology in Los Angeles, California, is an educational institution dedicated to the advancement of knowledge and the public appreciation of the Lower Jurassic. Like a coat of two colors, the museum serves dual functions. On the one hand the museum provides the academic community with a specialized repository of relics and artifacts from the Lower Jurassic, with an emphasis on those that demonstrate unusual or curious technological qualities. On the other hand the museum serves the general public by providing the visitor with a hands-on experience of "life in the Jurassic."

There immediately followed a small map, captioned "JURASSIC," which in every other respect looked exactly like a map of what the rest of us might refer to as Egypt. An arrow identified what in any other rendition would get called the Nile River Delta as "Lower Jurassic."

The text (which turned out to be the transcript of a visitor-activated slide show that ordinarily runs, accompanied by that same echt-institutional voice, in a small alcove over to the side of the entry—it just happened to be out of order that afternoon) went on to offer a treatise on museums in general:

> In its original sense, the term "museum" meant a spot dedicated to the Muses—"a place where man's mind could attain a mood of aloofness above everyday affairs." By far, the most important museum of antiquity was the great institution at Alexandria founded by Ptolemy Philadelphius in the third century before Christ (an en-

deavor supported by a grant from the Treasury). And no treatment of the museum would be complete without mention of Noah's Ark in which we find the most complete Museum of Natural History the world has ever seen.

And so forth. At times stupefyingly specific, at other times maddeningly vague, the text went on to trace the museological impulse through its dark oblivion in the Middle Ages on into its subsequent regeneration during the sixteenth and seventeenth centuries, when

collections of natural objects became as common as collections of works of art and often both such collections were housed in the same repository. One of the earliest printed catalogues of a collection is that "of all the chiefest Rarities in the Publick Theater and Anatomie-Hall of the University of Leyden" which appears to have been published in 1591, but the date seems to be a mistake for 1691.

Highlighting the singular collections of John James Swammerdam, Dr. Matthew Maty, Ole Worm (and his "Museum Wormianum"), and Elias Ashmole, the pamphlet went on to note how in the early days such treasure troves were the exclusive preserve of various social elites. For this reason, the pamphlet seemed to hold the late-eighteenth-century American painter Charles Willson Peale in particularly high esteem. His remarkable emporium in Philadelphia

was open to all peoples (including children and the fair sex). . . . Peale fervently believed that teaching is a sub-

lime ministry inseparable from human happiness, and
that the learner must be led always from familiar objects
toward the unfamiliar—guided along, as it were, a chain
of flowers into the mysteries of life.

"Rational amusement," the pamphlet explained, was the
Peale Museum's intent, but also, by a curious irony, its
undoing:

> Imitators sprang up almost at once. A collection of odd-
> ities, unencumbered by scientific purpose, was found to
> be good business. Tawdry and specious museums soon
> appeared in almost every American city and town.
> This unsavory tendency finally reached its peak with Bar-
> num, who in the end obtained and scattered the Peale
> collections.

The Museum of Jurassic Technology itself, the pamphlet
went on to explain, traces its origins to "this period when
many of the important collections of today were beginning to take shape." In fact, many of the exhibits in the
MJT, according to the pamphlet, were originally part of
smaller and less well-known collections, such as the
Devonian and Eocene. In the slide-show version, inspira-
tional music of a certain generic, oleaginous consistency
would now swell up as the narrative built toward its
close:

> Although the path has not always been smooth, over the
> years the Museum of Jurassic Technology has adapted
> and evolved until today it stands in a unique position
> among the major institutions of the country. Still, even
> today, the museum preserves something of the flavor of

its roots in the early days of the natural history museum—days which have been described as "incongruity born of an overzealous spirit in the face of unfathomable phenomena."

Glory to Him, who endureth forever, and in whose hand are the keys of unlimited Pardon and unending Punishment.

All of which helped, and didn't.

"Um," I tried again, after having finished the pamphlet, "but I mean, how specifically did this museum get started?"

"You mean *this* museum?" Wilson begged clarification.

Well, yeah.

"Oh," he said. "Well, the seed material, I guess you

could call it, for the current collection—the Flemish moths, for instance, the ringnot sloth—that exhibit's not up right now—a few of the others—came down to us through the collection of curiosities

Owen Thum, Owen Thum the Younger, and Hester Boxbutte Thum

originally gathered together by the Thums—that's Owen Thum and his son, Owen Thum the Younger, who were botanists, or I guess really just gardeners in southwestern Nebraska, in South Platte. In some ways their collection was like those of the old European nobility, only on a kind of homespun Midwestern scale."

When was this?

"Oh, in the first half of this century—say, the twenties for the father, and on into the fifties with Owen the Younger. But then a man named Gerard Billius essentially stole the material. It's a complicated story, but Billius was a man with money, also from Nebraska—in fact I think also from South Platte. I'm not positive, I could look it up. Anyway, he saw some value in the collection and he befriended Owen the Younger—who, let's face it, was a kind of bumpkin, not very sophisticated—and he got Owen the Younger to write a deed of gift to him, Billius, into his will. Billius was a lawyer. As the years passed, Owen the Younger and his wife, Hester, began to sense Billius's true nature and they tried to retract the deed but it had been written in such a way as to be unrevocable. After Owen the Younger's death, his wife, Hester, got into a terrible confrontation with Billius—she was trying to deed the collection over to the Nebraska Historical Society instead—and it all ended up with her drowned in her backyard pool under highly suspicious circumstances."

When did he say this was?

"Oh, this would have been in the late fifties. Anyway, so the collection went to Billius. Only, he quickly lost interest in it—I guess it turned out not to have the importance, or anyway the financial potential, he first saw in it. So then—well, I get a little hazy here, I've never been quite sure how it got from Billius to Mary Rose Cannon, or anyway to her family. I think maybe she was his grand-daughter or something—she's from Nebraska too, or maybe Texas. Anyway, though, she was a person whom we'd known indirectly for some time, and then about ten years ago she sort of gave the material over to us. A nice woman, although we've kind of lost touch. But anyway, that was the start."

It was also, as I would subsequently come to recognize, a quintessentially Wilsonian narrative: ornate, almost profuse, in some of its details, but then suddenly fogging over, particularly as one gets closer to the present. Such stories usually both perform and require a kind of leap.

What about the stink ants?

"Well, those we first heard about, let me see, I think it was on a PBS special actually, and we immediately realized we wanted to include a specimen in our collection. However, tracking one down proved incredibly difficult. None of the usual outlets had ever heard of them or could lay their hands on one. Finally we tried the Carolina Biological Supply Company in Portland, Oregon."

Carolina Biological Supply . . . *in Portland, Oregon?*

"Yeah," Wilson assured me. "And that's where we ran into Richard Whitten." He thereupon launched into another byzantine saga, this one about a certain phenomenally gifted bug amateur who had his own spectacular collections of beetles and butterflies but had all kinds of other qualities as well (he was a great lover of song and singing and had had a lifelong ambition to sing in the Mormon Tabernacle Choir and one day just piled his family into a van and headed to Salt Lake City, where he rented a tux and then secretly insinuated himself into the choir during one of their concerts—all kinds of other stories), and he was the only one anywhere who proved capable of laying his hands on any stink ant samples, and he kept the museum regularly supplied.

And how, for instance (by now I'd started choosing my words carefully) had Geoffrey Sonnabend and Madalena Delani, um, entered his life?

"Well, I first came upon Sonnabend when we were trying to expand an exhibit we used to have on memory. Those three empty portholes in the back of the museum—I don't know if you noticed them. Well, they used to contain an exhibit contrasting the memory theories of Plato, Aristotle, and Augustine. I myself tend to be pretty forgetful, so memory's always been an interest of mine. For instance, Plato suggests somewhere that memory is like an aviary inside your head, with all these birds flying around, such that you might reach in for a ringdove

and accidentally pull out a turtledove instead. And we represented that through a wax hand holding a stuffed bird. Anyway, we were planning to expand that exhibit with a fourth porthole, evoking the work of Her-

The Platonic conception of memory

mann Ebbinghaus, who was a great turn-of-the-century German researcher—in fact *revitalized* the whole field. He'd generate thousands of nonsense syllables, have people memorize series of them, and then chart the decay in their retention of the series, ending up with this kind of storehouse model. Fascinating work.

"So, anyway, I was at the University Research Library over at UCLA one day, leafing through their Ebbinghaus books, when I just happened to come upon Sonnabend's three-volume *Obliscence* the next call letter over. It seemed like nobody had looked into those books in ages, they hadn't been checked out in years, but I started reading—Sonnabend himself tells the story about the theory's genesis, about Madalena Delani and Iguazú Falls in the preface—and I was completely bowled over. In part, I suppose, it was the romance of this theory that seemed to foretell its own oblivion. And then, just a few days later, I happened to be listening to Jim Svejda's 'Record Shelf' program on KUSC, the local classical-music station, and he was doing a whole hour show devoted exclusively to Madalena Delani—that, for instance, is how I first found out about how she died. It was an incredible coincidence—in fact, everything associated with the story is like a tissue of improbable coincidences—how they almost met, how they didn't, what either of them were doing there at the Falls in the first place. And those kinds of coincidences are also a special interest of ours here at the museum. We contacted the Chicago Historical Society and a fellow there named Rusty Lewis helped us enormously, particularly with the Gunther connection. The whole thing just grew and grew."

It was getting late, time to be going and gone. I looked down at the pamphlet again, at the archaic head. What was the story with him?

"Oh, Mr. J? That's what my daughter calls him. He's sort of like our mascot, I guess."

And the "A, E, N" on the banner outside?

"Well, you may have noticed the line on top of the letters: that signifies negation or cancellation. So that the 'A, E, N' means *non*-Aristotelian, *non*-Euclidean, *non*-Newtonian. Sort of one of our mottoes."

As I was opening the door to leave, I once again noticed the diorama of the urn and the moths. What about that?

"Oh, that's a little urn surrounded by French moths—or, no, maybe Flemish, I'm not sure."

And what was the significance of the urn?

"It's just an urn. I don't think it means anything."

And that other diorama—the chemistry-set bottles?

"Oxide of titanium, oxide of iron, and alumina—those are the three chemical constituents of corundum, which forms the basis for all sapphires and rubies. Actually, we have the bottles out there because of the link to sapphires, which as you may know, have long been associated with qualities of faithfulness and endurance."

A FEW DAYS LATER I happened to be at the UCLA Library on another project when, half on a lark, I started riffling through the computerized card catalogue. "Ebbinghaus, Hermann," I typed in, and sure enough there rose up a slew of references (*"Memory: A Contribution to Experimen-*

tal Psychology, 1913," etc.). Then I typed in "Sonnabend, Geoffrey," and the screen churned for a while, before finally clocking in: "No record found." I went up to the reference librarian and asked whether there wasn't perhaps some more complete catalogue, one covering all the libraries in the system; and he gestured over toward the OCLC computerized database on his own desk, which covers not only all the libraries in the UC system but pretty much all the collections of any consequence in the entire country. He typed in "Sonnabend, Geoffrey," but once again the answer came back: "No record found." I subsequently called information in Chicago and asked for the Northwestern University Press, only to be told there was no listing for that either—which seemed odd until the operator pointed out that if it did exist, the press, like the university itself, probably would be listed under Evanston, not Chicago, and, sure enough, it was. But when I called them, they'd never heard of Sonnabend either. I called KUSC and asked for Jim Svejda; when he came on, I explained the situation, told him about the exhibit, and asked if he'd ever done a show about the singer Madalena Delani. He just laughed and laughed: never heard of her. I called information in Chicago once again and got the number for the Chicago Historical Society. Once I got through to them, I asked dubiously for Rusty Lewis, who, however, did turn out to exist. Had he ever heard of Charles Gunther? "You mean the candy tycoon?" he shot back, without missing a beat. He went on to confirm every single one of the exhibit's details about Gunther—his collection, the transplantation of the Libby Prison, the historic tables, even the snakeskin,

which remains in the Historical Society's collection to this day.

Back at the library I asked about the ethnographer Bernard Maston: "No record found." I asked about Donald R. Griffith: "No record found." For some reason, I tried that reference out by title too—*Listening in the Dark*—and this time I hit paydirt, except that the book had a different subtitle and its author was Donald R. Griff*in*, not Griffith. I went upstairs to look over the book's index but found no references to Maston, the Dozo, or any *deprong mori*. I went back downstairs and tracked down Griffin's most recent whereabouts; he appeared to have retired to Lexington, Massachusetts, where I in turn located his number and called him up. When I reached him I started out by explaining about the museum (he'd never heard of it) and its exhibit about Donald R. Griffith—"Oh no," he interrupted, "my name is Griffin, with an *n*, not Griffith." I know, I said, I know. I went on to ask him if he'd ever heard of a bat named *Myotis lucifugus*. "Of course," he said, "that's the most common, abundant species in North America. That's why we used it on all the early research on echolocation." Did its range extend to South America? Not as far as he knew—why? As I proceeded to tell him about the piercing devils and the thatch roofs, the lead walls and the X-ray emanations, he took to laughing harder and harder. Finally, calming down, he said, "No, no, none of that is me, it's all nonsense—on second thought you'd better leave the spelling of the name Griffith the way it is." He was quiet for a moment, before continuing, almost wistfully, "Still, you know, it's funny. Fifty years ago, when we were first proposing the existence of something like sonar in bats, most people thought that idea no less preposterous."

I don't know why, I just couldn't let the story go. I called information in Portland, Oregon, and asked doubtfully whether they had any listings for a Carolina Biological Supply. They did. I called the number and asked for Richard Whitten. The woman who answered said he no longer worked there, which was really too bad, because he was such a wonderful character, bless his heart. She went on to regale me, completely unbidden, with tales of his incredible beetle and butterfly collections and of his other passions, how he'd even managed to sing in the Mormon Tabernacle Choir—the whole thing. A couple of years ago, though, she explained, he and his wife had pulled up stakes and headed down to San José, Costa Rica, where they'd finally launched their dream project—a little museum entirely given over to displaying their marvelous collections. Whitten didn't have a phone down there, but he had sent up some clippings—did I have a fax machine? It happened that there was one where I was staying. I gave her the number, and a few minutes later, the clippings started coming through: rapturous reviews of the Whittens and their new Joyas del Trópico Húmedo (Jewels of the Rain Forest) museum. The pages kept eking out of the machine for some time, until the last one, at the bottom of which there emerged a photo of Richard Whitten himself, beaming contentedly amidst his butterflies.

He was playing an accordion.

∾ ∾ ∾

"HE NEVER EVER BREAKS IRONY—that's one of the incredible things about him." I was talking with Marcia Tucker, the director of New York's New Museum, about David Wilson. It turns out there's a growing cult among art and museum people who can't seem to get enough of the MJT. I seemed to encounter it everywhere I turned: the L.A. County Museum, the Museum of Contemporary Art (MOCA), the Getty . . . "When you're in there with him," Tucker went on, "everything initially just seems self-evidently what it is. There's this fine line, though, between knowing you're experiencing something and sensing that something is wrong. There's this slight slippage, which is the very essence of the place. And his own presence there behind the desk, the literal-minded way in which he earnestly and seemingly openly answers all your questions, his never ever cracking or letting you know that, or even whether, he's in on the joke—it all contributes seamlessly to that sense of slippage.

"I was at an international conference of museum people a while back in Germany—top people," she continued. "And he was there, the only one wearing a suit. And at a certain point, he got up to give his presentation about the history of museums in general and his own museum within that history. Completely straight—but he took that conference from the most ultraserious, smug, self-satisfied, pompous level onto this whole other level altogether—this sheer flight of fancy. The foreigners who were listening to the simultaneous translation—you could tell that they were having a hard time. And afterwards they were all coming over to me, very confused, and asking, 'What kind of thing is this Museum of Jurassic Technology?' And I'd answer, 'Well, what kind of thing does it seem like to you?' It was just like psychoanalysis. The museum affords this marvelous field for projection and transference. It's like a museum, a critique of museums, and a celebration of museums—all rolled into one.

"Listen," she concluded. "I consider the Museum of Jurassic Technology to be one of the great artistic treasures of the Western World." As with everything to do with the MJT, it was hard to tell whether she was kidding or not.

Ralph Rugoff, an L.A. art critic, has spent a lot of time thinking about the MJT. And one of the things he most likes about the place is the way it deploys all the traditional signs of a museum's institutional authority—meticulous presentation, exhaustive captions, hushed lighting, and state-of-the-art technical armature—all to subvert the very notion of the authoritative as it applies not only to itself but to any museum. The Jurassic infects its visitor with doubts—little curlicues of misgiving—that proceed to infest all his other dealings with the Culturally Sacrosanct. (Thus, for example, another critic, Maria Porges, once noted how "Wilson satirizes perfectly the tiresome, pedantic qualities of 'authenticating' scholarship. The copious footnotes and references and didactic panels are certainly fictitious, something I've long suspected of the citations in academic journals anyway.") "It's all very smart," Rugoff insists, "and very knowing."

Very knowing, and yet at the same time utterly sincere. Rugoff told me how one day he was sitting beside David's wife, Diana, at a lecture Wilson was giving to a class at the California State University, Los Angeles. It was an early version of his Sonnabend spiel, which in fact for a long time existed solely as a lecture, only relatively recently having taken on its exhibitional form. "And he did it completely straight," Rugoff recalls. "Everybody there was taking notes furiously, as if this were all on the level and was likely to be on the test—the Falls, the cones, the planes, the whole thing. It was amazing. And at one point I leaned over to Diana and whispered, 'This is the most incredible piece of performance art I've ever seen.' And she replied, 'What makes you think it's a performance? David *believes* all this stuff.' "

As I SAY, I began making a point of visiting the museum on each of my trips out to Los Angeles, and each time David would be there manning the desk, so that after a while I got to know him pretty well—which is to say, it felt like I got past the first layer of ironylessness to, well, maybe a second layer of ironylessness. I don't know. Occasionally we'd talk about his own life story, and it's my impression that everything he told me was more or less true-as-stated (or, anyway, whatever I could check did check out), although, as with some of the displays, a wealth of solid detail early on began to fog over somewhat as one approached the present.

David was born in Denver in 1946, the middle of three well-loved sons of a doctor (an ear, nose, and throat

specialist) and his wife. The family lived in the old subur-
ban neighborhood of Mountclair, originally founded as a
spa by one of the von Richthofens (either the baron himself or a close relative). The von Richthofen castle, allegedly an exact replica of the family manse back in
Germany, dominated a nearby hill, and in fact, directly
across the street from the Wilson's own home, the
founder had planted an elaborate memorial to his de-
ceased wife, featuring a very large and imposing urn into
which he had deposited her ashes. Already in those days
Denver had a brace of wonderful museums—natural history, oriental, state historical, art—and David recalls
how as soon as they could ride the buses unaccompanied,
he and a sidekick would travel downtown to spend the
day exploring among them. I asked him what had first at-
tracted him to the museums, and he replied, "Well, their
museumness. How dark and hushed they were inside, the
oak-and-glass cases, the sense of being in these reposito-
ries amongst all those old things. That, and the curious
style of writing—for instance, on the wall captions. Already then I was fascinated by what I've since come to see
as these curious ellipses, the jumps between what you as
a visitor are just assumed to know and the most minute,
often bizarre, detail of explication, a leap in rhetoric that
at times can be absolutely breathtaking. We've tried to
preserve a bit of that effect with some of the exhibits
here—for instance, the European mole. In fact, the caption for the ringnot sloth exhibit—one of our most arcane captions—is taken verbatim in its entirety from the
caption of a similar exhibit at the Field Museum in
Chicago. It's true. Nobody believes me."

∽∽   ∽∽

Prehistoric man must have known the extraordinary
Ringnot Sloth, although none of the numerous cave
paintings (such as those at Lascaux and Font-de-Gaume
in Southern France) appear to represent it. It was probably extinct by Roman times for, as Richard Owne noted
in 1846, "The total silence of Caesar and Tacitus re-
specting such remarkable animals renders their existence and subsequent extirpation by the savage natives a
matter of highest improbability." On the other hand, references to "Grimmer Schelch" in the Niebelungen Songs
would seem to indicate that this animal lived recently
enough to be mentioned in this bit of folklore.

∽∽   ∽∽

David was the kind of student who excelled when
challenged but whose performance fell off markedly
when he grew bored. From early on he displayed a passion for display—for instance, for building shoebox dioramas of Neolithic or American Indian scenes. He loved
the false perspectives, and he especially loved anything to
do with miniature light sources or optical instruments.
But he was hardly a recluse. In fact his mother recalls
how in his early years he was enormously gregarious, ex-
troverted, and social—a regular party animal.

Then something happened, although Wilson is loath
to talk about it; he gets all shy and hesitant (as opposed
to rhetorically opaque) at the prospect. "I really don't
know if I want to get into this," he says. "It's embarrassing, and it's hard to put into words without sounding in-
sipid or grandiose. But since you ask. . . . Sometime late
in high school—I was maybe seventeen or eighteen—my

parents and brothers were away for a week and I was home by myself, when out of the blue, for no reason, I underwent this incredibly intense psychological—how should I say?—well, like a conversion experience. It's just that I came to understand the course of my life and the meaning of life in general. Like that: as if in a flash. For instance, I knew that there would be no purpose for me in pursuing the world of acquisition. The experience had religious overtones to it, but not in any specific way. It was the most intense experience I've ever had—an entire week in awe and euphoria. It was as if I was receiving instructions. God—do I want to be talking like this? It's not so much that it's embarrassing, I just don't want to be doing the forces behind it a disservice. And I definitely don't want to claim any specialness. It was like something was being given to me—somewhere between a gift and an assignment—and one wants to be incredibly careful how one treats of such things.

"All at once it was made completely apparent to me, though without any detail, how my life would have to follow the course that has led to . . . well"—he gestured to the walls around him—"to this. I mean, I see running this museum as a service job, and that service consists in—I can't believe I'm saying these things—in providing people a situation . . . in fostering an environment in which people can change. And it happens. I've seen it happen.

"But without a doubt, that task was laid out for me in those days—the general structure was clear, even if it then took an extremely long time for me to be able to realize it; and that whole while, I sensed myself waiting, stumbling around on the forest floor, confused—like that ant."

He was quiet for a moment, then asked me not to publish any of the foregoing, or anyway not until he'd had time to reconsider. Of course I promised to defer to his wishes. (Eventually, if somewhat reluctantly, he did extend his permission.) I pointed out to him that I wasn't interested in performing any kind of exposé. After all, I said, it wasn't as if he were some kind of imminent danger to the body politic—

"Oh, I don't know," he interrupted me, smiling but at the same time deadly serious. "I like to think I am."

His mother confirms how somewhere late in his high school years David changed, became more serious, and she even lets on how maybe she preferred him the old way: "He was a lot more fun as a party boy than as a Chinese philosopher."

Soon thereafter he enrolled at Michigan's Kalamazoo College—a small, independent school patterned along the lines of Antioch, Oberlin, or Reed—where he ended up majoring in urban entomology with a minor in art. His first night there he met Diana at a square-dance mixer.

"I really get tired of all the leprechaun stuff," Diana once told me, referring to the press's penchant for dwelling on David's elfin, puckish, pixie aspects. "So I hesitate before abetting it any further. But what can I say? That first night—I was seventeen, and it was the end of my first full day at college, and we were all there square-dancing, and I do-si-do'd and turned to my left and there, facing me, was . . . well, this *gnome*. This old, small man. It was *scary*: he was only nineteen, but he was kind of ageless—or rather, *aged*. Still, I overcame that initial shock, and within a few days I could tell that he was also the most interesting guy there, and within a month I knew he was the man I would marry."

They were in fact married a few years later, in 1969, during the last weeks before their graduation. "Yeah," David acknowledges, "we've been married for twenty-five years. It's amazing—and believe me, every bit as amazing to us. We ought to be in one of our vitrines. But she's incredible," he continues, the ironylessness cracking just the slightest bit: "I can't believe how she puts up with all this."*

After college, David and Diana moved to Chicago, where almost immediately David was called up by his draft board. He applied for conscientious objector status, which, he says, "was granted in record time. They just looked at me and, no questions asked, I was like the dictionary definition. Diana says I really had the air of a religious fanatic in those days." He spent the next few years doing alternative service as an orderly in a mental ward and then in the emergency ward at the University of Colorado Hospital.

After that stint ended, he and Diana bought a lot in an extremely remote section of Colorado mountain country, and proceeded to build themselves a cabin in which they then managed to live for several years—no electricity, no water, a miles-long trek to the nearest road, necessities lugged in by ski over snow yards-deep during the winter months. ("We were desperately trying to avoid becoming yuppies," David recalls, "which was already a

---

* This and all subsequent asterisks refer to the Notes, which can be found at the back of the book, beginning on page 111.

distinct possibility.") And yet somehow, despite such primitive conditions, they managed, frame by frame, panel by panel, to eke out an entire animated film (David had become interested in film his last year at Kalamazoo), on the basis of which David was admitted to the newly opened California Institute of the Arts in 1974. (Within weeks of their reporting there, the Wilsons received word that the tenant to whom they'd rented their cabin had accidentally burned it to the ground. "Probably the best thing that ever happened to us," Diana acknowledges. "It meant we didn't have to go back.")

Cal Arts at the time was a hotbed of the coolest and most austere in formalist, avant-garde filmmaking, and David Wilson soon earned a reputation as one of the coolest, most austere filmmakers there. In the years thereafter, he became an important member of L.A.'s Film Oasis collective, regularly producing short films of an almost excruciating purity. It happens I even saw one of them, years ago, at an Oasis screening. I was utterly bowled over when, during the course of one of our recent conversations, I learned that David had been its creator, for it was a film that lived with me for a long, long time. It was called *Stasis* and lasted a bare thirteen minutes. What Wilson had apparently done was go out into the countryside and film a single long shot of a distant mountain stream. The camera started in tight, through a telephoto zoom lens, the stream and some overhanging trees filling the frame. Over the next thirteen minutes the camera pulled back, infinitesimally slowly, until by the end the lens probably took in the entire wide horizon, with the original stream and trees a tiny, indistinguish-

able speck in the middle of the image. Back in the lab,
however, over what must have been a period of many
months maniacally hunched over the optical printer,
David recut every single frame back to the original
composition of stream and tree, blowing the image up
as much as was necessary to fill the screen. The effect, in
the finished version of the film, was to watch as this
very crisp, clear, *substantive* image slowly, indefinably,
dematerialized into pure light and grain—and it was
mesmerizing.

First and last frames of David
Wilson's film Stasis

David was as surprised
as I was that I'd seen it.
"Well," he said, "it was the
kind of thing that was mod-
erately meaningful to a mi-
croscopically small percentage
of the population at a particular moment. But clearly, in
the end, it wasn't fulfilling
the mandate I'd received."
Diana, for her part, says flatly, "Those films were not
David." For one thing they languished in the self-select-
ing ghetto of an elite formalist audience, whereas David
was busy trying to interact with ("to service") a far wider
and more diversified clientele. (One of the things David
most treasured about those Denver museums was their
public character, the way they were open to any- and

everyone.) Still, from this distance, it's possible to sense a certain continuity between those early films and the more recent incarnation of David's vocation. There's the fascination with optical effects and equipment, of course. But more to the point, there's the sense of fascination itself. Only, whereas in his films it was almost purely the form itself that mesmerized, subsequently he's been able to achieve that same level of magnetized, riveting amazement through the manipulation of content. Your jaw drops almost as far whether it's facing *Stasis* or the stink ant vitrine; the difference is that by the time David was producing his museum vitrines, he'd found a way to lace that sense of fascination with a distinct undercurrent of perturbation.

David continued making his formalist films through the seventies and into the early eighties, and though obviously he wasn't making any money off of them, he and Diana were nevertheless able to enjoy a very comfortable lifestyle because they were making so much money on the side doing highly sophisticated and specialized camerawork (for example, with motion-control robotic animation) on the periphery of the film industry (TV commercials, special effects, industrial films, promotional sequences for the network sweeps). "It was the sort of work you could do six months a year and easily coast the rest of the time," David says, "and I even enjoyed it. Technically, it was quite challenging and interesting. But it wasn't the kind of work where you were adding beans to the right side of the scale. It wasn't even so much who you found yourself working for, though sometimes that could give you pause—at one point we were doing some industrial work for some of the coal company villains in Harlan County—as the way we were relentlessly contributing to the constriction in people's attention spans, and the sense that thematically . . . Face it, in that kind of work you can count the themes you engage on the fingers of one hand, even if you don't have any arms."

His other life, however, was already opening out. In 1980, Terry Cannon, who ran the Pasadena Film Forum, the region's premier avant-garde venue, approached David with a proposition. The theater was going to be dark over the summer, and David could have the place's lobby to do with as he pleased. Rising to the challenge with tremendous enthusiasm, David created a sequence of four exquisitely evocative, dreamlike vitrine-dioramas, each of them fronted by a stereoscopic viewing device modeled on the catoptric (or so-called beam-splitting) camera. The visitor would gaze into the diorama through a viewfinder into which, via an intricate array of prisms and mirrors, David was able (as with the bridge over Iguazú Falls) to seamlessly project a free-floating video loop—of an angel mysteriously appearing and disappearing, for example, amidst the cottony cloudscape of the underlying diorama. The lobby was simply open to

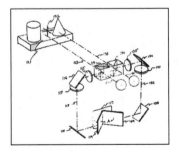

the public during daylight hours, and whoever happened to be walking by could partake of the experience, or not. Many people

Catoptric camera

did, and all kinds of different people: the show had wonderful word of mouth. This was much closer to the mandate, as David quickly realized, and increasingly he began
producing other sorts of cabinet splendors and farming
them out to various odd venues.

And it's here that David's account begins to fog over.
His own biography intermeshes with the museum's. The
Thums make their appearance, via Terry's wife, Mary
Rose Cannon, who either was or wasn't Gerard Billius's
granddaughter.* Within a few years David would be oc-
cupying his Culver City storefront, but there would be a
lot of shape-shifting in between—a catoptric confla-
tion—and it's a bit difficult to achieve a strictly accurate
chronological account, at least from him.

Diana, for her part, tells the story of how one day in
1984, just before she got pregnant and around the time
she was waiting to hear whether she'd been admitted to
graduate school, she'd just finished a Tai Chi class when
David drove over to get her. Upon pulling up, he waited
for her to board the car, at which point he passed her a slip
of paper upon which he'd scrawled the simple phrase,
"Museum of Jurassic Technology."

"What's this?" Diana asked him. "Your life's work?"

And he just smiled.

FOR ITS FIRST SEVERAL YEARS, the Museum of Jurassic
Technology existed in the form of "loans from the Collection" extended to scattered galleries, museums, and
community centers—it had no physical base of its own.
Then one day, about seven years ago, while driving home

from his other life's professional studio in Culver City, David noticed that a nearby storefront he'd had his eye on for some time had suddenly gone vacant. (Before that it had served as a fireworks factory, a sheepskin outlet, and, most recently, as an overflow storeroom for the neighboring forensics lab.) David signed a lease on the spot, taking over the 1,500 square feet. ("When we first moved in," he recalls, "we had to clear out thousands of little blocks of wax with samples from people's bodies embedded inside.") Within a few months he'd reunited his museum's traveling diaspora, mounted his first exhibition, and without the slightest flash or ceremony, simply hung the banner out and opened up for business.

Passersby, on occasion, would wander in. Many would wander right back out. But some would stay and linger. David tells the story of one fellow who spent a long time in the back amidst the exhibits and then, emerging, spent almost as long a time studying the pencil sharpener on his desk. "It was just a regular pencil sharpener," David assures me, "it wasn't meant to be an exhibit. But he couldn't get enough of it." And he tells another story about an old Jamaican gentleman named John Thomas who also spent a long time in the back and then came out crying. "He said, 'I realize this is a museum but to me it's more like a church.'" David seems equally—and almost equivalently—moved by both stories. (In a way, they're the same story.) Occasionally visitors are moved to offer more substantial financial contributions to the museum, and along a wall in the foyer there's an engraved honor roll acknowledging the support of these patrons in much the same spirit of parody mingled with reverence that characterizes most everything else about the museum. Other visitors began volunteering their services to sit at the desk or else to help fabricate the new installations. In talking about the museum, David continually defers authorship: he is always talking about "our" goals and what "we" are planning to do next. In part this is one of his typical self-effacing gambits; but it's also true that the museum has generated a community—or anyway, that it's no longer so much about what's going on "inside" David as about what's going on "between" him and the world.*

That it continues to persist at all from month to month is by no means the least of its marvels. "The museum exists against all odds," David once commented to me. "Nothing supports this venture—it is woven from thin air. We apply for grants, and we've gotten a few, but most grants-dispensing agencies frankly don't know what to make of us. We don't fit into the traditional categories." (I've seen some of those applications and I'm not sure I'd know what to make of them either: as I say, David never breaks irony, and in these applications he always presents the museum as a straightforward public-educational institution much like any other—only, with some really odd enthusiasms and a penchant, shall we say, as one of its reviewers once parsed the matter with exquisite delicacy, for presenting "phenomena known to science, if known at all, because of their appearance in the museum itself.") The museum's annual budget currently hovers around $50,000 (rent is $1,800 a month, and no one receives a salary), and though David originally poured a significant portion of his own outside income into the museum, there's been less and less of that, in part because as the years passed he spent more and more time on the museum itself, and in part because his exquisitely sophisticated battery of specializations has now largely been superseded by the film industry's relentless computerization. Have there been moments, I recently asked him, when he and his family have actually been at the poorhouse door? "Oh, yeah," he laughed. "Moments like now."

"I have no idea how we got this far or how we can possibly go on," Diana told me one day. Technically she's the museum's treasurer and keeper of accounts, though she admits that in that official capacity she's often reduced to giggling fits. "I've just developed this faery-faith in last-minute providence. At the outset of each month, there's no way we're going to make it through, but something always comes up—a small bequest, a grant unexpectedly approved, a slight uptick in admissions. Actually, we're just about reaching the point where admissions may soon be covering the rent. But David keeps pushing the limit. Last year he took his other company into bankruptcy and doubled the size of the museum *on the same day*—and the crazy thing is, *I wanted him to do it!* He was right to do it. And we got lucky, because almost immediately after that my car got stolen, so we were able to pour the $6,750 settlement from that into the museum."

She was silent for a moment. "But it's strange, because less than a decade ago we were on the cusp of the upper middle class. The other day our daughter DanRae asked me, 'Mommy, are we poor?' I told her, 'Yes, but not without hope.' "

DanRae, incidentally, seems far from anxious. Nine years old, she's as blithely self-confident and unabashed as her parents are tortuously shy and deferential. She's also *big*. "Beats me," David laughs when asked about the disparity. "Sometimes, maybe, it's just that two negatives make a positive." (Her given name is Daniela Rae. "The 'Rae' is after Diana's dad, Raymond, who died when she was still a young girl," David explains. "The 'Daniela' is for Joseph McDaniels, the gynecologist who told Diane she'd never be able to bear children. Wonderful man. Just proved to be wrong in that one particular instance.") I've heard stories about how five years ago DanRae used to curl up for long naps on the floor of the museum's darkened back alcoves. Nowadays she bounds around like she owns the place. When asked at school what her father does, she simply replies, "Oh, he's got a museum." And she often brings classmates over for tours. One day she escorted me around, pointing out which exhibits were really cool and which other ones were, frankly, pretty boring. She squeezed through the glass partition and into the *deprong mori* showcase to show me a particularly nifty bug from out of a drawer in Bernard Maston's portable study desk. In the Madalena Delani room, she pointed into the glass case at one of the diva's pearl bracelets and confided, "That was my necklace when I was a baby." For her, the museum is the most natural thing in the world.

ONE OF MY FAVORITE EXHIBITS at the Museum of Jurassic Technology, the "FRUIT-STONE CARVING," consists of a simple glass box hanging from the wall at eye level. Inside, atop a thin spike pedestal and under perfect illumination, is displayed—well, some kind of fruit pit, I guess. It's about the size of a dime, and it seems like it's been somewhat haphazardly gouged out. It's hard to tell: there's no magnifying device. There is a tiny square mirror attached to the tip of another thin spindle, this one jutting out from the wall, and it affords a view of the back of the hollowed pit. The nearby wall caption reads as follows:

Almond stone (?): the front is carved with a Flemish landscape in which is seated a bearded man wearing a biretta, a long tunic of classical character, and thick-soled shoes; he is seated with a viol held between his

Fruit-stone carving
at the MJT

knees while he tunes one of the strings. In the distance are representations of animals, including a lion, a bear, an elephant ridden by a monkey, a boar, a dog, a donkey, a stag, a camel, a horse, a bull, a bird, a goat, a lynx, and a group of rabbits: the latter under a branch on which sit an owl, another bird and a squirrel.

On the back is shown an unusually grim Crucifixion, with a soldier on horseback, Longinus piercing Christ's side with a lance; the cross is surmounted by a titulus inscribed *INRI*. Imbricated ground.

Dimensions: Length 13 mm.
Width 11 mm.

Maybe. As I say, it's hard to tell: it looks like an ordinary pit. It would be nice if there were a magnifying device, though, what with the Iguazú Falls eyepiece around the corner, with its phantom catoptric bridge, I'm not sure that even then one would credit the evidence of one's own eyes.

That was certainly the case with another recent show at the museum, consisting of thirty cylindrical acrylic display cases each of which contained a single needle mounted beneath a twenty-five-power magnifying device. The wall captions alleged that suspended within or alongside the eyes of each of the needles were thirty microminiature sculptures. And sure enough, gazing through the eyepieces, one could spy variously: Little Red Riding Hood; a determined-looking Napoleon; Donald Duck (with orange bill, blue jacket, and yellow-webbed feet); a waving John Paul II in full papal regalia; Snow White and all seven of her dwarfs (microminiature dwarfs, that is). There was even one of Christ himself stretched out upon a golden cross. One of the displays gave its name to the entire show. It was titled "A Wish upon a Piece of Hair," and the accompanying caption claimed that the artist had etched the wish onto a strand of his own hair. A hair was

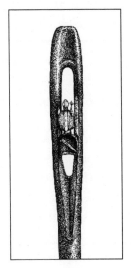

Drawing of Hagop
Sandaldjian's
microminiature
sculpture of Pope
John Paul II

there, and it distinctly read, "May all your dreams come true."

According to the wall legends, these were all the work of a single Soviet-Armenian émigré violin instructor, by the improbable name of Hagop Sandaldjian, who'd painstakingly crafted them under a microscope out of motes of dust, specks of lint, and wisps of hair, using tools he'd fashioned himself (mostly exquisitely sharpened needles tipped with abrasive ruby and diamond dusts), and then colored them by applying minute amounts of paint in microscopic suspension with paintbrushes consisting of a single hair. When I asked David about Sandaldjian, he assured me that he must have been "a very calm man." In fact he claimed to have known him briefly, having first heard of his existence from a visitor to the museum. He explained how he'd thereupon taken to visiting Sandaldjian at his home in the Montebello section of East L.A., but how, no sooner had he contrived a plan for showing the sculptures at the Jurassic than, calling Sandaldjian to tell him so, he received word from his son that the master had died not ten days prior. Of course, they went ahead with the show anyway.

That show was no longer up but it had been replaced, as it were, by another equally mind-boggling display, this one supposedly documenting recent achievements in microtechnology. "NANOTECHNOLOGY," announced the wall panel, "Machines in the Microscopic Realm"—and an array of microscopes mounted along a long table proceeded to afford visitors glimpses of what indeed appeared to be precisely what their captions alleged: a wobble motor, a microspring, micro-machined inter-

An instance of nanotechnology:
pressure sensors on the head of a pin

meshing gears ("gear tooth approx. the
size of a red blood cell"), an electrosta-
tic motor, and even a micro wind tun-
nel. The captions credited these achievements to various
inventors with names like "Yu Chong Tai, California Institute of Technology," and "A. Bruno Frazier, Georgia
Institute of Technology"—but, as I say, you could never
be sure.

Or anyway, I couldn't. So I called the California Institute of Technology and asked the campus operator for
Yu Chong Tai, and sure enough, she put me through, and
a voice answering to that name proceeded to confirm
everything my eyes had seen. "And more's coming!" it assured me. That conversation in turn made me doubt my
earlier doubts about the dubious Sandaldjian. I called information in Montebello, where it turned out such a family did indeed reside. And I ended up speaking with the
master's son, Levon, who explained that there was in fact
something of a tradition of such microminiature art
back in Armenia (he knew of two or three other such instances), although, as far as he knew, his father had been
the world's only microminiature *sculptor*. "He would wait
until late at night," Levon said, "when we kids were in bed
and the rumble from the nearby highways had subsided.
Then he would hunch over his microscope and time his
applications *between heartbeats*—he was working at such
an infinitesimal scale that he could recognize the stir-

rings of his own pulse in the shudder of the instruments he was using."

THOSE EARLIEST MUSEUMS, the ur-collections back in the sixteenth and seventeenth centuries, were sometimes called *Wunderkammern*, wonder-cabinets, and it occurs to me that the Museum of Jurassic Technology truly is their worthy heir in as much as wonder, broadly conceived, is its unifying theme. ("Part of the assigned task," David once told me, "is to reintegrate people to wonder.") But it's a special kind of wonder, and it's metastable. The visitor to the Museum of Jurassic Technology continually finds himself shimmering between wondering *at* (the marvels of nature) and wondering *whether* (any of this could possibly be true). And it's that very shimmer, the capacity for such delicious confusion, Wilson sometimes seems to suggest, that may constitute the most blessedly wonderful thing about being human.

I RECENTLY HAD OCCASION to raise this point with John Walsh, the director of the Getty Museum and another fan of the MJT. We were talking about *Wunderkammern* and some of the museum's other antecedents. "Most of the institutional-historical allusions at Wilson's museum turn out to be true," Walsh told me. "There *was* a Musaeum Tradescantianum and a John Tradescant—in fact two of them, an Elder and a Younger—who during the 1600s built up a famously eclectic cabinet known as 'The Ark' in Lambeth on the South Bank, in London, most of the contents of which devolved to Elias Ashmole, who expanded upon them and then donated the whole collection to Oxford University, where it became the basis for the Ashmolean. There was a Swammerdam in Holland, and there was an Ole Worm with his Museum Wormianum in Copenhagen; and Charles Willson Peale did have his museum in Philadelphia, to which Benjamin Franklin donated the carcass of his angora cat and where you could also see the huge skeleton of a recently unearthed mastodon, and mechanical devices like the Eidophusikon, which showed primitive movies.

"Ever since the late Renaissance," Walsh continued, "these sorts of collections got referred to as *Kunst- und Wunderkammern.* Technically, the term describes a collection of a type that's pretty much disappeared today— with the exception, perhaps, of the Jurassic—where natural wonders were displayed alongside works of art and various man-made feats of ingenuity. It's only much later, in the nineteenth century, that you see the breakup into separate art, natural history, and technology museums. But in the earlier collections, you had the wonders of God spread out there cheek-by-jowl with the wonders of man, both presented as aspects of the same thing, which is to say, the Wonder of God."

I asked Walsh about some of the relics and bizarre curiosa that used to make it into those collections right alongside the legitimate stuff: the hair from the beard of Noah, the plank from the Ark, the women's horns. I mentioned how I always figured some of those early museum men must have been being ironical in including them.

"Well," Walsh said, "there's a whole big side industry

in twentieth-century criticism that consists primarily in the imputing of irony to prior ages. But no, no, I don't think they were being ironical at all. They were in dead earnest."

I WAS TALKING with David in the back room of the museum one afternoon on one of my most recent visits out to L.A. It was a weekday and the museum was closed, and he'd been showing me slides of some utterly unknown, never previously shown paintings by a complete recluse who, he told me, was suffering the ravages of multiple sclerosis—protean, fantastical vistas of astonishing intricacy. He was thinking about giving them an exhibition. Our conversation turned to Sandaldjian. Free-associating, I mentioned the Talmudic story of the Thirty-six Just Men—how at any given moment there are thirty-six ethically just men in the world, unknown perhaps even to themselves, but for whose sake God desists from utterly destroying the shambles we have made of His creation. Maybe, I suggested, there are thirty-six *aesthetically* just men, as well.

David looked at me, authentically noncomprehending. "I don't understand the difference," he said.

He was quiet a few moments, and once again the ironylessness seemed momentarily to crack. "You know, certain aspects of this museum you can peel away very easily, but the reality behind, once you peel away those relatively easy layers, is more amazing still than anything those initial layers purport to be. The first layers are just a filter . . ."*

He was quiet another few moments, and just as surely I could sense that the crack was closing up once again, the facade of ironylessness reasserting itself inviolate.

I mentioned the stink ant.

"See," he said, "that's an example of the thing about layers. Because at one level, that display works as pure information, as just this incredibly interesting case study in symbiosis, one of those adaptations so curious and ingenious and wonderful that they almost lead you to question the principle of natural selection itself—could random mutation through geologic time be enough to account for that and so many similar splendors? Nature is more incredible than anything one can imagine.

"But at another level," David continued, "we were drawn to that particular instance because it seemed so metaphorical. That's another one of our mottoes here at the museum: *'Ut Translatio Natura'*—Nature as Metaphor. I mean, there've been times in my own life when I felt exactly like that ant—impelled, as if possessed, to do things that defy all common sense. That ant is me. I couldn't have summed up my own life better if I'd made him up all by myself."

"But, David," I wanted to say (and didn't), *"you did make him up all by yourself!"*

SHORTLY AFTER, back home in my office, I was in a phone conversation about something entirely different with Tom Eisner, the eminent biologist up at Cornell. At one point, in passing, he told me about a trip he'd taken to Italy, many years ago, and how, while in Pavia, a colleague had given him a tour of the ancient university's old museum. At one point, as they foraged among the back rooms, the colleague pulled out a glass jug containing some organs bobbing in a dusky fluid solution. " 'You'll never guess what this is,' my friend challenged me," Eisner related, "and I didn't even try. *Lazzaro Spallanzani's cock and balls!'*" I'm not sure whether Eisner took my silence on the other end of the line for scandalized astonishment or tongue-tied ignorance, probably (more correctly) the latter. "Spallanzani was one of the great early modern naturalists," he offered helpfully. "Eighteenth century. He was the first, for instance, to isolate spermatozoa in semen, did some wonderful experiments on gastric digestion (feeding bits of meat tied to string to various birds of prey, letting the string descend only so far, and then yanking the string back out with the meat completely liquified and gone, thereby proving that large portions of digestion take place in the stomach and not in the bowels, as had previously been assumed), all sorts of splendid things.

"Anyway, my colleague recounted for me how during one of the sieges of Pavia—Pavia always seemed to be coming under siege in those days—Spallanzani realized that he was dying of some urinary-tract infection; he kept careful notes on the progress of the disease and authorized an autopsy after his death so that his colleagues could study the bladder and kidneys themselves. Only, his corpse fell into the hands of his sworn enemy and fiercest rival, I forget the guy's name, an anatomist—in my own mind I always think of him as Scarpia, as in *Tosca*. So anyway, this Scarpia extracted not only Spallanzani's

bladder and kidneys but his entire reproductive apparatus as well, which he thereupon proceeded to display with
considerable glee. Remember: this is Italy, and such public emasculation was just about the worst affront to a
man's honor that could be imagined. So that years later,
after Scarpia died, Spallanzani's old students got ahold of
his corpse, decapitated it, and preserved the head in a jar
of its own, which to this day rests on a shelf in the museum right nearby Spallanzani's."

Eisner laughed and then fell silent for a few moments,
perhaps marveling at the sheer passion of his forebears.
"But Spallanzani was great," he resumed, "had all kinds of
great intuitions. Some of his work refuting the idea of
spontaneous generation was a good half of the way toward Pasteur. He bred eels. He was into bats: poured wax
in their ears to see if that would affect their navigational
abilities . . ."

At this point the coincidences were becoming just too
bizarre. I mentioned Wilson's museum (Eisner had never
heard of it) and in particular its exhibit about Bernard
Maston, the *deprong mori*, and Donald Griffith—"That's
Griff*in*," Eisner interrupted, "with an *i-n*, not a *t-h*." I
know, I said, I know. "Funny about Griffin," Eisner continued. "He's a great scientist too, and a dear friend of
mine. In fact, years ago, as a graduate student at Harvard,
I inherited my first lab from him. There was still this
wonderful weird grid of holes drilled into the walls,
holes which had once held the anchors onto which he'd
attached the maze of wires crisscrossing the room which
formed the basis for his original research proving that
bats could navigate in the dark. That lab had a marvelous

history. Immediately before Griffin it had been occupied by the Alfred Kinsey who did such terrific groundbreaking work on reproduction among the cynipid wasps— that is, before he abandoned the field entirely to concentrate on human sexuality instead."

I read Eisner some passages from the *deprong mori* brochure and he laughed and seemed to love them. "That's wonderful," he said, not the least bit miffed. "That's exactly what it's like when you're out there in the field and you're first encountering some of those marvelously strange natural adaptations. At first all you've got is a few disconnected pieces of raw observation, the sheerest glimpses, but you let your mind go, fantasizing the possible connections, projecting the most fanciful life cycles. In a way it's my favorite part of being a scientist— later on, sure, you have to batten things down, contrive more rigorous hypotheses and the experiments through which to check them out, everything all clean and careful. But that first take—those first fantasies. Those are the best."

I decided to try the stink ant out on Eisner. Wait until you hear this, I told him, this one is even funnier. Whereupon I proceeded to read him the first few paragraphs of this very piece right off my computer screen. He listened attentively, audibly harumphing his concurrence every few sentences. "Yup," he said. "Yup . . . yup." When I'd finished, he said, "So, where's the joke? All of that stuff is basically true."

I was struck almost speechless. Really? I stammered.

"Oh, absolutely. I mean, I don't know the names exactly—they're not precisely my field, so I'm a little rusty on those ants. But let's see: *Megaloponera foetens*, you say? I don't think *Megaloponera* exists, but there is a genus that used to go by the name *Megaponera*, although—it gets a little complicated—lately I'm told it's been folded into another category called *Pachycondyla*. And there is an African ant called *Pachycondyla analis.* '*Foetens'* is smelly, but '*analis'*—well, let's just say that's even more smelly. And I believe that that ant does stridulate—it's not a cry exactly, but it does produce this faint chirping sound. As for whether *Pachycondyla* ingests the spore that way, I'm not sure. But there are several other species that do, some of them right here in the United States. For instance, down in Florida there's an ant, *Camponotus floridanus*, which inhales or anyway somehow takes in spores of the *Cordyceps* fungus, and occasionally you will indeed come upon those ants, far from home, high up the stalk of some tall blade of grass, for instance. Their mandibles will be clamped onto the blade and they'll be quite dead, a long, thin, curved pink candlestick-like protrusion growing out from their head. And that's the fungus, getting set to shed spores. No, no," Eisner laughed, delighted. "That's all true. Just goes to show: nature is incredible. No way—*no way*— this could all have been created in just six days." (That was great: every bit as wonderstruck as Wilson, Eisner had derived exactly the opposite evolutionary conclusion from the likes of the stink ant.) "In fact," he continued, "wait a second, I think—yeah—my wife, Maria, and I photographed one of those a while back down in Florida. You got a fax?"

I gave him the number.

"Just a second," he said, and rang off.

And sure enough, a few moments later, a photo of a dead *Camponotus floridanus*, his forehead gloriously rampant, came coursing up from out of my machine.

Camponotus floridanus *with* Cordyceps *fungus*
as photographed by Tom and Maria Eisner

PART II

Cerebral Growth

Centaur recently excavated near Volos, Greece

After an earlier, abridged version of the foregoing essay appeared in the September 1994 issue of *Harper's*, the magazine got some wonderful letters. One fellow from Chicago saw fit to alert the editors to a possible fraud, noting that "The weight of five solid lead walls, eight inches thick, twenty feet high and two hundred feet long calculates out at 9,154,000 pounds. If each person on [Griffith's] eight-month expedition to the Tripsicum Plateau in South America carried fifty pounds of lead (plus sensors, etc.), that equates to 190,280 assistants."

To which the only proper response would have to have been: "So? Still doesn't prove it couldn't've happened."

Other correspondents, meanwhile, offered observations and clippings about parallel sorts of enterprises to David Wilson's. For example, I was sent an article about an exhibition of "The Centaur Excavations at Volos," according to which three centaur skeletons with bones dating to "1300 B.C. plus or minus three hundred years" were unearthed in 1980 "at Argos Orestiko, eight kilometers northeast of Volos, Greece." One of these skeletons forms the centerpiece of the exhibit, still embedded in a slab of Greek sandstone displayed under glass along a long wooden flatbed table: eerie the way the horse's spinal column courses seamlessly into the arched vertebrae of the human torso. Looking closely, you can even make out the rusted barb of the arrow that pierced the monster's human heart. The show's curator, William Willers, an artist and biology professor at the University of Wisconsin in Oshkosh, is quoted as explaining how "Such centaurs roamed the Thessalian woods until they met men's arrows and spears, then fled into the hills, where cold and hunger did the rest."

(But *is* there even a University of Wisconsin in *Oshkosh?*)

Other letters reminded me, for example, of Donald Evans's epic project, an enchantingly evocative and spectacularly executed philately of an entirely imaginary alternative world. The American artist (b. 1945) collated hundreds of these sublime (and exceedingly rare, if not downright unique) postage stamps, from such countries as the Isle des Sourds, Antiqua, Domino, Amis and Amants, Lo Stato di Mangiane, My Bonnie, Nadorp, Pasta, and the Republica de Banana, before his own untimely passing in 1977 as the result of a fire in his Amsterdam flat. Others mentioned Charles Simonds, the urban archeologist who first began uncovering (or discovering, or deploying—it was never quite clear) the exquisite diminutive ruins left behind by various wandering tribes of "Little People" (their fastidiously layered walls fashioned out of red clay bricks only millimeters long) amidst the crumbling hollows of various tenements in Lower Manhattan—this was during the early seventies (Simonds's work has in the meantime graduated off the streets and into some of the world's premier galleries, from Seoul to Barcelona, from the Guggenheim to the Jeu de Paume). Back in the early seventies, Norman Daly, a professor emeritus at Cornell, elaborated an entire fictional civilization, known as "Llhuros," from which he was even able to exhibit more than 150 artifacts.

One of the most energetic of such enterprises currently under way, to which I was likewise alerted by several correspondents, is the Hokes Archives at the University of Tennessee in Knoxville, originally founded in London by Everett Ormsby Hokes (1864–1939) but currently under the directorship of Beauvais Lyons, an associate professor of art at the university and himself the explicator of no less than three previously unheard-of civilizations: the Arenot of North Central Turkey, the Apasht from the Hindoo Kush of Afghanistan, and the Aazud of Mesopotamia. (The Arenot, for example, were "a dystopian society" with "an extremely dualistic cosmology." According to one interpretation, they believed that "because copulation is necessary to the creation of a life, ritual necrophilia is the only means to create the afterlife." Prevalent among the imagery one is able to spot among the Arenots' surviving pottery shards is the so-called dog-eat-dog motif, a canine-cannibalistic daisy chain, as it were.)

Among other documents accompanying a letter from the Hokes Archive's own assistant director was a Selected Bibliography, which featured, among other things, a reference to Norman Daly's seminal text "Possible Aazudian Origins of Llhuroscian Culture" from Vol. 118, no. 2, pp. 121–32 of the *Bulletin of Llhuroscian Studies* (London, 1962). The letter itself, meanwhile, also noted how "a literary paradigm for the Hokes Archive" can be found in the fiction of Jorge Luis Borges, and specifically in his 1941 story "Tlön, Uqbar, Orbis Tertius" (included in his book *Ficciones*), in which a secret society is discovered to be painstakingly confabulating an entire encyclopedia documenting the physical and intellectual legacy of an otherwise long-lost culture, though reference to this civilization also appears to have seeped into at least one copy (Borges's own) of Volume XLVI of the *Anglo-American Cyclopedia*. Borges further claims that he has in the meantime also been able to secure a single volume—*XI: Hlaer to Jangr*—from the secret society's *First Encyclopedia of Tlön.**

The letter went on to note how Mr. Lyons was by no means alone in this pursuit and how indeed last year he'd organized a symposium bringing together several other such like-minded academic visionaries, a sort of "conference paper version of *Zelig*," the letter said. It concluded by referring to my original *Harper's* piece and noting how I'd managed to "touch on the central issue regarding parody, how irony is signaled. David Wilson, Beauvais Lyons and many others working in this genre cultivate a deadpan sensibility in presenting this work. The tension between what is real and imaginary is a source of its aesthetic tension as well as its subversive implications. Additionally, the work is ultimately playful. One could wax on about this, but I'll let you draw your own conclusions."

I liked that last formulation and decided to telephone the letter-writer so as to further pursue its implications (the letter had been written on the archive's stationery, which provides both phone and fax numbers); in fact, I'd even begun dialing before I did a double take on the assistant director's name—Vera Octavia (not bloody likely)—and at long last grogged the resonances of the archive's own name as well. (Hokes!?) Thinking better of my initial impulse, I hung up without completing the call.

MEANWHILE, it was to other, much earlier, incarnations of David Wilson's museum that I began to turn my own increasingly obsessive attentions. John Walsh's allusions to *Wunderkammern* lodged in my brain like a spore and increasingly, in the midst of various other sorts of research forays, I found myself drifting over to those sections of the library that documented the early history of what would subsequently become museums. Walsh himself helped exacerbate these tendencies by sending me a marvelously daffy volume from the Oxford University Press entitled *The Origins of Museums: The Cabinet of Curiosities in Sixteenth- and Seventeenth-Century Europe,* a compendium of almost insanely recondite scholarly papers delivered at a 1983 conference called to celebrate the tercentenary of the opening to the public of Oxford's own Ashmolean Museum by the then Duke of York (subsequently King James II). It was in its pages, for instance, that I first came upon Francis Bacon's prescription for the essential apparatus of the compleat "learned gentleman" (from his *Gesta Grayorum* of 1594), and particularly his suggestion that in attempting to achieve within "a small compass a model of the universal made private," any such would-be magus would almost certainly want to compile "a goodly, huge cabinet, wherein whatsoever the hand of man by exquisite art or engine has made rare in stuff, form or motion; whatsoever singularity, chance and the shuffle of things hath produced; whatsoever Nature has wrought in things that want life and may be kept; shall be sorted and included."

That formulation—I especially liked the "singularity, chance and the shuffle of things" part—neatly anticipated the sorts of lists one comes upon everywhere in this vein of research. The *Origins* book, for example, cites the case of Bacon's contemporary, Sir Walter Cope (d. 1614), a politician and member of the Elizabethan College of Antiquaries, whose Kensington castle featured, according to the 1599 diary of a Swiss visitor named Thomas Platter, "an appartment stuffed with queer foreign objects in every corner," including, among other things: holy relics from a Spanish ship Cope had helped to capture; earthen pitchers and porcelain from China; a Madonna made of feathers, a chain made of monkey teeth, stone shears, a back-scratcher, and a canoe with paddles, all from "India"; a Javanese costume, Arabian coats; the horn and tail of a rhinoceros, the horn of a bull seal, a round horn that had grown on an Englishwoman's forehead, a unicorn's tail; the baubles and bells of Henry

VIII's fool, the Turkish emperor's golden seal . . . (Another diarist, a few years later, noted the addition of such recent acquisitions as "a passport given by the King of Peru to the English, neatly written upon wood," and a little Indian bird, phosphorescent by night.)*

By the late sixteenth and early seventeenth centuries, this sort of hoard (the chamber of wonders, in which the word *wonder* referred both to the objects displayed and the subjective state those objects inevitably induced in their respective viewers) was rampant all over Europe, and the question arises: Why? Or rather, why *then?* To say that such wonder was an essential aspect of early Renaissance experience merely begs the question: What was it about the early Renaissance that provoked such an avalanche of wonder? And of course the answer, as Platter's awestruck inventory of Cope's treasure trove itself suggests, lies in the avalanche of marvelous new *stuff* that had suddenly begun pouring over the transom into a previously parochial, hidebound, closed-in European subcontinent. In particular, the stuff of the New World.

That, in turn, is the theme of Stephen Greenblatt's masterfully evocative study *Marvelous Possessions: The Wonder of the New World* (1991). "Wonder," Greenblatt argues, was "the central figure in the initial European response to the New World, the decisive emotional and intellectual experience in the presence of radical difference." And this was something new. "*Nil admirari*, the ancient maxim taught," as Greenblatt continues. "But in the presence of the New World the classical model of mature, balanced detachment seemed at once inappropriate and impossible. Columbus's voyage initiated a century of

*America in the marveling eye of Europe: Theodor de Bry's
depiction of Indian hunting stealth (Frankfurt, 1590)*

intense wonder. . . . European culture experienced something like the 'startle reflex' one can observe in infants:
eyes widened, arms outstretched, breathing stilled, the
whole body momentarily convulsed."*

At one point Greenblatt scrutinizes a passage from the
French Huguenot pastor Jean de Léry's great *History of a
Voyage to the Land of Brazil* (1578, but based on travels
of two decades earlier) in which Léry recalls a particularly unsettling and exotic evening among the Tupinamba natives in the Bay of Rio, concluding, "Whenever
I remember it, my heart trembles."* This trembling,
Greenblatt glosses, "is the authentic sign of wonder," for
"wonder, as Albertus Magnus wrote, is like 'a systole in
the heart.' . . . Someone witnesses something amazing,

but what matters most is not 'out there' . . . but deep within, at the vital emotional center of witness."* The fact that Léry doesn't have a clue as to what the Tupinambas' rituals actually signify *for them* renders his own experience of that evening, and its subsequent recollection, all the more powerful, for himself. As the historian Michel de Certeau has written, "An absence of meaning opens a rift in time." And that experience—of the ground opening before one's feet—was at the heart of the sensation of wonder ideally afforded by (or at any rate striven toward in) many of the cabinets of the time. *That* was the spirit, the taste of the age. (And the fault line runs clear through, from there to the Museum of Jurassic Technology.)

As Greenblatt goes on to observe, "The expression of wonder stands for all that cannot be understood, that can scarcely be believed. It calls attention to the problem of credibility and at the same time insists upon the undeniability, the exigency of experience."

At the outset of his own account (Greenblatt points out), Léry asks how his French readers can be made to "believe what can only be seen two thousand leagues from where they live; things never known (much less written about) by the Ancients; things so marvelous that experience itself can scarcely engrave them on the understanding even of those who have in fact seen them?" (Bernal Díaz, who accompanied Cortés on the conquest of Mexico and subsequently recorded the adventure in his *The Conquest of New Spain*, at one point similarly recalls the Spaniards' first spellbound vision of the Aztec capital: "Gazing on such wonderful sights, we did not know what to say, or whether what appeared before us was real.") In Guiana in the 1590s, Sir Walter Raleigh began hearing native reports about people in the interior with "eyes on their shoulders and mouths in the middle of their breasts." Raleigh knows his readers may take this for "a meere fable," the sort of thing with which Sir John Mandeville (d. 1372) was wont to fill his accounts of travel to the Far East and which earned him such a reputation as a liar. But for Raleigh, as Greenblatt notes, it is skepticism rather than credulity that is likely to be misleading: "Such a nation was written of by Mandeville, whose reports were holden for fables many yeeres, and yet since the East Indies were discovered, we find his relations true of such things as heretofore were held incredible." Léry makes the same point about even earlier authors, noting how while he is still hesitant to believe everything he reads, nevertheless, ever since visiting America, "I have revised the opinion I formerly had of Pliny and others when they describe foreign lands, because I have seen things as fantastic and prodigious as any of those—once thought incredible—that they mention."

The point is that for a good century and a half after the discovery of the Americas, *Europe's mind was blown.* That was the animating spirit behind, and the enduring significance of, the profusion of *Wunderkammern.** It wasn't just the American (or, alternatively, African, Far Eastern, Greenlandian, etc.) artifacts that they displayed (phosphorescent feathers, shrunken heads, rhinoceros horns). It was how the palpable reality of such artifacts so vastly expanded the territory of the now readily conceivable. Horns, for example, were suddenly all the rage—rhinoceros horns, unicorn horns, *sea* unicorn horns . . . human horns, dainty round horns coming sprouting out of proper Englishwomen's foreheads, for God's sake! But rhinoceros horns *were* real; and sea unicorns *did* exist (in the form, anyway, of narwhals, with those uncannily spiraling unitary tusks seemingly protruding from out of their foreheads)—so why couldn't unicorn horns or even human horns exist as well? Our great-grandfathers' certainties, debunked by our grandfathers, were suddenly turning out to be not quite so easily debunkable after all.*

Obviously the mathematical and navigational sophistication necessary for Columbus to have been able to mount an expedition to America—and then make it back, and not once, but four times!—was of a considerable level, and was indicative of a steadily rising curve of such certain, positive knowledge (the earth wasn't flat, and there clearly weren't any sea monsters lurking along its edge to swallow up any stray doubters). But the stuff he found in America, and the stuff he brought back, was so strange and so new as to seem to sanction belief in all manner of wondrous prospects and phantasms for years thereafter.

So that collections, every bit as catholic and deliriously heterodox as Cope's—to judge from the frontispieces gracing their respective eventual catalogues—began sprouting up all over Europe: the Tradescants' in Lambeth, Francesco Calceolari's in Verona, Ole Worm's in Copenhagen, Ferrante Imperato's in Naples, Manfredo Settala's in Milan, Athanasius Kircher's in Rome. In some instances, the main guiding principle of accumulation,

Francesco Calceolari's museum in Verona (1622)

echoing Bacon's injunction, seemed to reflect a sort of Noachian passion: ideally, one or two of every single thing in the world—"the universal nature made private." (As far as that ambition was concerned, an inside track perhaps belonged to Father Kircher, who, as a leading German scholar based at the Jesuit College in Rome, was able to draw on the order's farflung contacts and resources all over the world.)

Often there seemed to be no order whatsoever to the pell-mell pile, or none discernible to us, save that of continuous, compounding amazement. Adalgisa Lugli, a contemporary Italian art historian, writing on "Inquiry as Collection" and referring to lists such as Platter's (she's obviously been exposed to a good many of them in the course of her work), notes wryly how the seventeenth-century museum "was still conceived of as a place where . . . one could move about without having to solve or face the problem of continuity." (Arthur MacGregor, an assistant keeper at the Ashmolean, and one of the editors of the *Origins* volume, strikes a similar note of straight-faced hilarity in describing how "Rudolf II [1552–1612] established at the Hradschin Palace in Prague one of the most impressive artistic centers of his time. As well as being an outstanding patron, Rudolf built up a truly remarkable collection which has frequently been likened to his own personality in its immense richness and lack of purposeful direction.")

Sometimes a sort of taxonomical order was imposed upon the hoard, though one which might seem oddly arbitrary to modern sensibilities: At the Anatomical Museum in Leiden, for example, specimens in one corner were grouped by *type of defect*, such that separate pickling jars containing two-tailed lizards, doubled apples, conjoined Siamese twin infants, forked carrots, and a two-headed cat were equably ranged side by side. (Of course, the point is that these were themselves the very years when the so-called modern sensibility, with its own eventual taxonomical imperatives and conventions, was in the hit-and-miss process of taking shape.) Other times, a sort of moral order was overlaid across the material. Note, for example, how the pelican atop the shelf to the right in

Imperato's museum (see back endpaper of this book) has been stuffed and mounted as if stabbing itself with its own beak (and indeed, this appears to be the very thing that's caught the attention of the courtiers inside the picture as well). This detail doubtless refers to the belief, pervasive at the time, that pelicans were given to tearing their breasts open so as to resuscitate their dead young with their own blood, a contention first adumbrated by Pliny the Elder (A.D. 23–79) in his *Natural History* but one which naturally dovetailed quite nicely with subsequent Christian iconography. The curious thing here, of course, is that the taxidermist in question, who in all likelihood never himself saw an actual live pelican, chose to confabulate precisely that scripturally resonant posture for the animal's display in his natural history museum.

The Dutch in particular seemed partial to such moralizing presentations. As early as the 1590s, the Theatrum Anatomicum in Leiden housed a veritable emporium of rearticulated skeletons, both animal (ferret, horse) and human. In many cases the human skeletons, as accompanying banners proclaimed, proved to be those of executed criminals (a cattle thief's skeleton, for instance, was mounted astride the skeleton of an ox). The centerpiece of the entire amphitheater, meanwhile, consisted of a woman's skeleton offering an apple to a man's beneath a scraggly Tree of Knowledge. Nearby, pennants bearing archly moralizing inscriptions on the terrible consequences of original sin drove home the necessary lessons for any dim souls who might still have been missing the point.

This moralizing tenor persisted throughout the sev-

Interior of Theatrum Anatomicum, Leiden (1610)

enteenth century in Holland, reaching an astonishing
crescendo in the Baroque labors of the great Amsterdam
anatomist Frederik Ruysch, whose collection of over two
thousand meticulous presentations eventually filled up
more than five rooms in his home. Some of his tableaux
were relatively straightforward: the skull of a prostitute,
for instance, being kicked by the leg bones of a baby.
Some were heartrending: Ruysch had perfected ways of
preserving the entire bodies of dead infants in large glass
jugs in presentations that were often lavished with extraordinary and loving care (the serene, stilled faces swathed
in delicate lace, the limbs banded with prim beaded
bracelets). Some were peculiar: Ruysch proudly exhibited

One of Frederik Ruysch's vanitas mundi *tableaux,*
Amsterdam (early 1700s)

a box of fly eggs taken from the anus of "a distinguished gentleman who sat too long in the privy" (Ruysch's own description from his catalogue). And some were downright bizarre: his masterworks, perhaps, were a series of *vanitas mundi* tableaux, exquisite skeleto-anatomical variations on traditional flower arrangements grouped around the theme of life's inevitable transience. For their base, Ruysch would contrive a mound of kidney stones and other diseased organs—this in itself was not that unusual since dried kidney and gallstones (the bigger, the better) were regularly featured in wonder-cabinets all over the continent. But then, on top of those . . . well, consider the contemporary engraving by C. Huyberts, as explicated more recently by Dr. Antonie Luyendijk-Elshout of the University of Leiden, based on Ruysch's own notes:

With eye sockets turned heavenward the central skeleton—a foetus of about four months—chants a lament on the misery of life. "Ah Fate, ah bitter Fate!" it sings, accompanying itself on a violin, made of osteomyelitic sequester with a dried artery for a bow. At its right, a tiny skeleton conducts the music with a baton, set with minute kidney stones. In the right foreground a stiff little skeleton girdles its hips with injected sheep intestines, its right hand grasping a spear made of the hardened vas deferens of an adult man, grimly conveying the message that its first hour was also its last. On the left, behind a handsome vase made of the inflated tunica albuginea of the testis, poses an elegant little skeleton with a feather on its skull and a stone coughed up from the lungs hanging from its hand. In all likelihood the feather is intended to draw attention to the ossification of the cranium. For the little horizontal skeleton in the foreground with the familiar mayfly on its delicate hand, Ruysch chose a quotation from the Roman poet Plautus, one of the favorite authors of this period, to the effect that its lifespan had been as brief as that of the young grass felled by the scythe so soon after sprouting.

Sadly (I guess), none of Ruysch's *vanitas mundi* tableaux appear themselves to have survived the ravages of time, though many of his other preparations have—although, curiously, for the most part, not in Holland. Ruysch (who, incidentally, for all his preoccupation with frail mortality, himself managed to survive into his ninety-third year, in 1731) fairly late in his life sold virtually his entire collection to the Russian tsar Peter the Great, which is why students wishing to survey Ruysch's superb craftsmanship in person today must travel to St. Petersburg.*

TSAR PETER'S PURCHASE of Ruysch's collection, along with many others, in 1717, was an attempt to amass, ex nihilo, a vast *Wunderkammer* of his own—another of his many attempts to modernize the Russian Empire in one fell swoop. Ironically, however, the universalizing ambitions and wildly heterodox tastes which undergird such a venture were already beginning to seem anachronistic in the face of the onrushing Enlightenment, with its penchant for a more skeptical, vigorous, and systematically delineated type of order. Half a century later, Peter's granddaughter-in-law, Catherine the Great, wrote to a curator who still favored the old style: "I often quarreled with him [Peter] about his wish to enclose Nature in a cabinet—even a huge palace could not hold Her." And, to a degree, during her reign she allowed Peter's cabinet to molder (meanwhile herself amassing, in the more modern style, a huge collection of over four thousand paintings and then erecting a vast palace, the Hermitage, within which to house them). For that matter, Ruysch himself was a transitional figure between one world that seems entirely foreign to us and another that begins to feel much more recognizably our own. (Indeed, his own work was instrumental in helping to shape that latter world; a recent biographer has described him as "probably the most skilled and knowledgeable preparator in the history of anatomy.")

For well more than a century before that, however, the sense of wonder afforded a steady undertow to any simple, straightforward advances in positivist certainty.* And in fact it had to be beaten back—by Galileo and Newton and Spinoza and Descartes—before that steady positivist advance could once again forge forward, unimpeded. ("What we commonly call being astonished," wrote Descartes, who wanted to get people out of their hearts and back into their heads, where they belonged, "is an excess of wonder which can never be otherwise than bad.") And by the mid-1700s, the age of wonder was indeed giving way to the Enlightenment, with its bracing sense of steadily accumulating scientific certainty and progress, a sense of the world that would in turn retain its hegemony, largely unchallenged, right up until the dawning of our own era—until, say, Newton slammed into Heisenberg.

In her essay "Inquiry as Collection," Adalgisa Lugli details many of the contemporary neopositivist objections to the *Wunderkammer* sensibility but then goes on to assert that such *Wunderkammer*-men as "Della Porta, Cardano and Kircher were not alone among men of science [of their time] in looking upon wonder or marvel as upon one of the essential components of the study of nature and the unraveling of its secrets . . . wonder defined [as it was up to the end of the eighteenth century] as a form of learning—an intermediate, highly particular state akin to a sort of suspension of the mind between ignorance and enlightenment that marks the end of unknowing and the beginning of knowing."

Over two centuries later (on the far side of Heisenberg's new dispensation), according to James Gleick in his introduction to Richard Feynman's recently reissued *Character of Physical Law*, "Physicists had hands-on experience with uncertainty and they learned how to manage it. And to treasure it—for the alternative to doubt is authority, against which science fought for centuries. 'Great value of a satisfactory philosophy of ignorance,' Feynman jotted on a piece of notepaper one day, 'teach how doubt is not to be feared but welcomed.' This became his credo: he believed in the primacy of doubt, not as a blemish upon our ability to know but as the essence of knowing."*

David Wilson has thus pitched his museum at the very intersection of the premodern and the postmodern—or rather, perhaps what he has done is to tap into the premodern wellsprings of the postmodern temper.*

FOR A BIG BOOK, *Tradescant's Rarities* sure wasn't easy to find. Published in 1983 as a sort of companion volume to *The Origins of Museums*, *Tradescant's Rarities*, according to the notice on the backflap of the *Origins* volume, consisted in a study of the collections that had constituted the foundations for the Ashmolean Museum itself, along with a catalogue listing. For some time I'd harbored a vague interest in perusing that list, partly because of the number and quality of the references to the Tradescants in other sources—but also, no doubt, because of some of the references to the Tradescants in several of Wilson's more farfetched exhibits, such as that of the horn of Mary Davis of Saughall—so that every once in a while I'd casually check the inventories of any libraries I happened to be using for other projects, but the volume never showed up, not until one day when I managed to track it down in the backstacks among the art-book holdings at the Forty-second Street Branch of the New York Public Library.

Opening the volume to its preface, my glance casually strayed over to the copyright statement on the facing page:

© Ashmolean Museum, Oxford 1983
Published in cooperation with the Visitors of the Ashmolean
by the Delegates of the Press

Just above, the Oxford University Press's address was given as "Walton Street, Oxford, OX2 6DP," and below that came an equally familiar (though entirely different) litany of place names:

London   Glasgow   New York   Toronto
Delhi   Bombay   Calcutta   Madras   Karachi
Kuala Lumpur   Singapore   Hong Kong   Tokyo
Nairobi   Dar es Salaam   Cape Town
Melbourne   Auckland
and associates in
Beirut   Berlin   Ibadan   Mexico City   Nicosia

The first essay in the book, authored by the volume's editor Arthur MacGregor, was entitled "The Tradescants:

Gardeners and Botanists." And indeed much that followed was similarly familiar: the Tradescants—John the Elder and John the Younger—were, like the Thums, primarily gardeners and botanists (the Elder had even been appointed Keeper of His Majesty's Gardens, Vines, and Silkworms at Oatlands Palace). The father died in 1638, after which the son continued his labors, further expanding the marvelous collection based in their home, known

*John Tradescant the Elder, Elias Ashmole, and
John Tradescant the Younger with his wife, Hester*

as the Ark, in Lambeth. The son married a young woman named Hester, but when *their* son died they began casting about for another means of transmitting the family's bounteous legacy to posterity. During the early 1650s they were befriended by one Elias Ashmole, an ambitious gentleman of considerable social standing—he was Comptroller of the Excise, an astrologer regularly consulted by the king, author of several historical and alchemical works, and a founding member of the Royal Society.

On one of their first outings together, Ashmole and John the Younger traveled to Maidstone to attend a witchcraft trial. In 1652, Ashmole began cosponsoring an inventory and cataloguing of the Ark's entire collection. "Following publication of the catalog in 1656," MacGregor reports, "our knowledge of Tradescant stems mainly from legal documents, such as the deed of gift of 1659 by which the collection of rarities was assigned to Ashmole, and the recensions in two subsequent wills." For, indeed, the Tradescants did try to revoke that clause in their will, though Ashmole, perhaps owing to his superior legal training, had managed to frame its original wording in such a way that it could only be revoked through the mutual consent of both parties. Even after John the Younger's death in 1662, his widow strove mightily, through a succession of "unhappy lawsuits much disturbed," to wrest the collection from Ashmole's clutches, though these efforts ceased in 1668, after she was discovered mysteriously drowned in her own pond.*

Thus, the preposterously unlikely saga of the Thums and Gerard Billius turns out to be the very foundation tale behind one of the foremost collections in England today. Ashmole, for his part, deeded the collection to Oxford University, where he had briefly studied, with a stipulation that the building containing the collection become the site, as well, for a "school" for the study of natural history, or "philosophical history," as it was then known—England's first. (Like his contemporary Frederic Ruysch—or, for that matter, countless other contemporaries, including Isaac Newton himself—Ashmole was a man with one leg planted in the prior world of shaggy superstition and the other striding confidently toward the new era of systematic science; and indeed, the seat of the Tradescant collection, itself so emblematic of that earlier era of indiscriminate wonder, thus became a principal locus, over the next several centuries, for that wonder's domestication and standardization.)*

The story of the Tradescants, for that matter, bore out many of Stephen Greenblatt's assertions as well. As gardeners and botanists, both father and son were far-flung fieldworkers—the father traveling as far as Muscovy and Algiers, the son to Virginie itself, in their ongoing efforts to bring back and introduce novel plant species to the English countryside. It was in the very course of these travels that they first began compiling their own cabinet of wonders, and it was the fame of that cabinet (and of their gardens) which in turn garnered them the contacts necessary to enlist other travelers in their collecting efforts. A wonderful letter, dated 1625, from Tradescant the Elder (writing on behalf of his new patron, the Duke of Buckingham), to Edward Nichols, the then–Secretary of the Navy, begins: "Noble Sir,"

> I have Bin Comanded By My Lord to Let Yr Worshipe
> Understand that It Is H Graces Plesure that you should
> In His Name Deall withe All Merchants from All Places
> But Espetially the Virgine & Bermewde & Newfownd
> Land Men that when they Into those Parts that they will
> take Care to furnishe His Grace Withe All maner of
> Beasts & fowells and Birds Alyve or If Not Withe Heads
> Horns Beaks Clawes Skins Fethers . . .

and so on and so forth, culminating in a list of more
specifically desired items, which included, among others:

> on Ellophants head with the teeth In it very large
> on River horsses head of the Bigest kind that can be
>   gotton
> on Seabulles head withe horns
> All sorts of Serpents and Snakes Skines & Espetially of
>   that sort that hathe a Combe on his head Lyke
>   a Cock
> All sorts of Shining Stones or of Any Strange Shapes

finally concluding, succinctly:

> Any thing that Is strang.

And as MacGregor's various ensuing citations from letters written by various contemporary visitors to the Ark
attest, the Tradescants had indeed collated a whole bunch
of things that were "strang."* There are frequent references to human horns, for example, though all such supposed horns (including that of Mary Davis of Saughall)
have in the meantime unaccountably, though perhaps not
surprisingly, disappeared.

MacGregor quotes a Georg Christoph Stirn who, in

describing the collection, as he observed it in 1638, noted, among other items: two huge ribs from a whale (out in the courtyard); "a goose which has grown in Scotland on a tree"; "a number of things changed into stone" (in other words, fossils, which in other such collections often get referred to as "picture stones"); the hand of a mermaid; the hand of a mummy; a small piece of wood from the cross of Christ; "pictures from the church of S. Sophia in Constantinople copied by a Jew into a book"; "a bat as large as a pigeon"; an instrument "used by Jews in circumcision"; the robe "of the King of Virginia"; a girdle such as the Turks wear in Jerusalem; "the passion of Christ carved very daintily on a plumstone" . . .

That last reference, to the crucifixion of Christ daintily carved on a plum stone, brought me up short as I sat there hunched over Stirn's letter amidst the field of worktables at the New York Public Library. It set me to riffling through the back pages of MacGregor's catalogue, with its detailed inventory of all the rarities from among the Tradescants' collections that have survived among the Ashmolean's holdings to this day. (Along the way I came upon a map of the Siege of Pavia, the very same one that graces Wilson's wall at the museum, followed by no less than *fourteen columns* of scrupulous scholarship explicating the tiniest details of a painting depicting the 1534 siege that had gotten included in Tradescant's collection—Fig. 74, Cat. no. 263.) Eventually, to my astonishment, I came upon the following:

181. FRUIT STONE CARVING (PL. LXXXVI)
Almond stone (?): the front is carved with a Flemish landscape in which is seated a bearded man wearing a

biretta over long hair, a long tunic of classical character, and thick-soled shoes; he is seated with a viol held between his knees while he tunes one of the strings, framed by the branches of a tree. The back is filled in with representations of animals, including a lion, a bear, an elephant ridden by a monkey, a boar, a dog, a donkey, a stag, a camel, a horse, a bull, a bird, a goat, a lynx, and a group of rabbits: the latter under a branch on which sit an owl, another bird and a squirrel.

Dimensions: Height 25 mm; Width 22 mm.

182. FRUIT STONE CARVING (PL. LXXXVI)
Plum-stone (?) relief. On the front is shown the Crucifixion, with a soldier on horseback, Longinus piercing Christ's side with a lance, and other mounted horsemen behind; to either side of the cross, surmounted by a titulus inscribed *INRI*, stand the Virgin and St. John, and a skull lies below. Imbricated ground.

Dimensions: Height 23 mm; Width 19 mm.

And indeed, Plate LXXXVI showed the very same. Not only had such wonders been perpetrated (and as early as the 1600s!), but in Oxford, today, they still exist, open to inspection, at any time, by any stray pilgrims from the Jurassic.*

Tradescant fruit-stone carvings, actual size

∾ ∾ ∾

DURING MY MOST RECENT visit to L.A., David Wilson and
I agreed to rendezvous for lunch at the little India Sweets
and Spices mart, with its deli-style take-out counter, a few
doors down the block from his museum. Walking in, I
was greeted by the familiar blast of sinuous aromas—
David and I had repaired to this place several times before—only, this time, it was as if my recent investigations
had hypersensitized me to its special qualities. I took in
the prodigious bounty of its exotic offerings—such fresh
vegetables as the eggplant-like brinjal, spiny kantola,
beany valor, green tuver, tindora, lotus root, and chholia
(easily the oddest looking of them all); all manner of teas
and fragrant herbs (from coriander and cardamom
through the curry powders); packaged ajwan seeds and
Vicco brand vajradanti paste; curried arvi leaves, stuffed
brinjal, karela in brine; enticing trapezoidal wedges of
dessert cakes like the gold-and-silver-foil-laced almond
barfis . . . I had this sudden sense of what it must have
been like to have been sitting there, all closed in, in the
cold, damp, monotone, monobland Europe of the 1400s,
as little by little all this wild, wonderful stuff began pouring in (initially, at least, by way of overland caravans),
how easy it would have been to be overwhelmed by such
exquisite new delicacies: *We've got to get more of this stuff!*
We've got to find an easier way of getting it! We've got to get
ourselves over there! Standing there, waiting for David, for
a moment I felt like I was planted in the very engine room
of history.

    David eventually showed up and we ordered our

marsala dozas, pekoras, and cardamom teas and took them out to the little picnic tables out front, facing the boulevard. We spoke about India and the fantasy of the Indies and the impulse, the *orientation* toward wonder. One thought led to another. I'd been about to comment on how incongruous it was to find a sixteenth-century *Wunderkammer* like his in the middle of Los Angeles, California, when suddenly it dawned on me—why not? In fact, Los Angeles was one of the most appropriate places in the world for such an enterprise.

After all, back in the sixteenth and seventeenth centuries, California was awash with Europeans agog for wonder—and plunder. The name itself, as I subsequently discovered, appears to have derived from an old Spanish novel, *Las Sergas de Esplandián* (The Exploits of Esplandián), written in about 1510 by Rodríguez de Montalvo. The book itself was apparently nothing much to write home about, but there's considerable evidence that many of the conquistadors of the time were familiar with its story, in which Esplandián, a kind of late-medieval ideal knight, is helping defend Constantinople from a motley crew of pagan invaders when suddenly there appears amongst the besieging horde: Calafía, Queen of California. California, for its part, turns out to be an island "on the right hand of the Indies" and "very near the terrestrial paradise," inhabited by a race of Amazonian warriors whose weapons are of purest gold, "for in all the island there is no other metal"—all of which must have sounded pretty intriguing from the conquistadorial point of view. On the other hand, in California, according to Rodríguez, there were also "many griffins on account of the great ruggedness of the country"; when the griffins were small, "the women went out with traps to take them to their caves, and brought them up there. And being themselves quite a match for the griffins, they fed them with the men whom they took prisoners, and with the boys to whom they gave birth." So it was a mixed bag.

In 1542, exactly fifty years after Columbus's first landfall in the Caribbean, Juan Rodríguez Cabrillo led a fairly ragtag band aboard two small, leaky vessels well up the coast of Alta California, anchoring variously at San Diego, Catalina Island, San Pedro Harbor, which he called the Bay of Smokes *(Bahía de los Fumos)* on account of the many Indian campfires along its shore, and then in Santa Monica—not half a dozen miles from where David and I now sat wolfing down our pekoras and sweet lahsis—before heading up the coast toward Santa Barbara and San Miguel Island. A bit over thirty-five years later, in 1579, Sir Francis Drake came streaking by in his *Golden Hind* from the other direction, out of Point Reyes up north, heading down toward Cape Horn and then home, leading only the second expedition ever to circumnavigate the globe (and becoming the first captain of such an expedition to make it home alive, Magellan having died in the attempt). Once back in England, Drake lived on until 1596, when the Elder Tradescant would have been about twenty years old and certainly familiar with the legendary privateer's exploits. Years later, Tradescant's collection would include not only a portrait of Drake but also a "Trunion" from his ship.

Sitting there at the picnic table outside the Indian market, gazing west down Venice Boulevard, David and I fancied how, but for the smog, we could almost have made out the galleon traffic coursing by. At length we returned our trays and headed back to the museum, though entering this time from the rear, into David's workroom, which was brimming over with the half-completed vitrines of his next show, set to open in just a few weeks.

"Tell the Bees . . .: Belief, Knowledge and Hypersymbolic Cognition," a coproduction, according to its advance literature, of the MJT and the Society for the Restitution of Decayed Intelligence, had been in the works for years and was clearly going to be one of Wilson's most elaborate ventures to date. By way of introduction he suggested I don a pair of earphones and listen to the audio portion of the slide show that was going to accompany the exhibit while he continued to tinker with some of the vitrines. Once again, the production qualities of the tape were first-rate, blending subtle music, crisp sound effects, and a solid-seeming narration. The Voice of Institutional Authority started out by recounting the tale behind Alexander Fleming's 1929 discovery of penicillin; presently we were given what purported to be Fleming's own voice, or anyway a Scottish voice of raspy, wire-recorder quality, recalling how at the climactic moment of the accidental experiment, "It was found that broth in which the mold had been grown, like the mold-broth remedies commonly applied to infections by the country people, had acquired marked inhibitory, bactericidal, and bacteriolytic properties to many of the more common pathogenic bacteria." The wire was rewound and the phrase "like the mold-broth remedies commonly applied to infections by country people" repeated, whereupon Institutional Authority noted how in making his epic discovery, "Fleming was drawing on countless years of collective experience which had been handed down as a part of the oral tradition . . . commonly known as vulgar remedies." There was more on Fleming (how his familiarity with the vulgar remedy of spitting on a wound had earlier in his career led to his isolation of lysozyme, "an enzyme found in tears and saliva that exhibits antibiotic activity"), after which the narration turned to digitalis, the cardiac stimulant derived from a plant of the figwort family known as purple foxglove, which had already been deployed as a vulgar remedy for dropsy for centuries before it was "discovered" by William Withering, an eighteenth-century English physician, acting "on a tip from a wise woman from Shropshire." There were similar revelations about the vulgar etiologies of lithium and aspirin. "Belladonna, Madagascar periwinkle, and ipecac, to name just a few, are all vulgar remedies that have been recognized and developed by modern pharmacology."

At which point, the Voice of Institutional Authority darkened as it related how this once honored form of knowledge presently came to be denigrated, particularly in eighteenth- and nineteenth-century medical academies, where "Folk remedies were viewed as baneful influences, irrational relics from the past to be purged," so much so that much irreplaceable wisdom, "ghettoized, so to speak, under the spurious classification of superstition," has already been irretrievably lost. Hence the urgency animating the current exhibition, which was casting itself—although it would never have come right out and made such claims on its own behalf—as nothing less than a clarion call to the heroic enterprise of reclamation.

Amidst the sounds of waves and a distant foghorn, the narrative voice advised that "In order not to be set hopelessly adrift in this seemingly endless sea of complex and interrelating beliefs, this exhibition has limited its discussion to five areas of inquiry: Pins and Needles; Shoes and Stockings; Body Parts and Secretions; Thunder and Lightning; Insects and Other Living Things."

Thus we were once again tending into quintessentially Jurassic territory, having launched out on manifestly solid ground only to find ourselves . . . well, not really having any idea where the hell we were finding ourselves. The Voice was now explaining the title of the show, which drew on funeral practices dating back to Hellenistic Greece, when bees were understood to be "the muse's bird" and hence needed to be apprised of all major family events. There were elaborate rituals involving youngsters and beehives; and "there are a great many other practices that are observed concerning bees," the Voice continued. "Among those who know them well, bees are understood to be quiet and sober beings that disapprove of lying, cheating, and menstruous women. Bees do not thrive in a quarrelsome family, dislike bad language, and should never be bought or sold." And so on.

Finally, with the chorus of Pergolesi's *Stabat Mater* swelling in the background, the Voice concluded: "Like the bees, from which this exhibition draws its name, we are individuals, yet we are surely, like the bees, a group, and as a group we have, over the millennia, built ourselves a hive, our home. We would be foolish, to say the least, to turn our backs on this carefully and beautifully constructed home, especially now, in these uncertain and unsettling times."

Uncertain and unsettling, it occurred to me, were two good and apt words. I put down the earphones and quietly began drifting among the half-finished display cases. (Wilson, over in the corner at his workbench, completely involved in his labors, seemed to have become entirely oblivious of my presence.)

One apparently finished case contained a vial of an exquisite amber liquid alongside a curious little brush, like a toothbrush, only with metal bristles. Its caption read:

URINE

Like spittle, urine has beneficial or protective qualities, and clearly one of the most efficacious and widely practiced counter-charms involves the combination created by the practice of spitting into one's urine.

On New Year's Day it is a common practice for the oldest woman in the family, employing a small brush, to sprinkle with urine the household animals and then, individually, the members of the family as they are getting out of bed.

Another vitrine featured a wax face into whose mouth the bill of a stuffed duck's head protruded:

DUCK'S BREATH

Children afflicted with thrush and other fungous mouth or throat disorders can be cured by placing the bill of a duck or goose in the mouth of the afflicted child for a period of time. The cold breath of the fowl will be inhaled by the child and the complaint will disappear.

The duck's breath cure

David subsequently explained to me how he wasn't quite happy with that exhibit yet. The wax face looked too old and he was intending to cast his daughter DanRae's face in its stead—he just hadn't gotten around to doing it yet. (Didn't there use to be a surrealist comedy troupe named The Duck's Breath Mystery Theater? I decided not to ask.)

There was a large, ominously elegant-looking pair of scissors (actually a pair of old-fashioned sheep shears, I subsequently learned), mounted upright, and David was apparently trying to rig a mechanism inside the display's chassis that would allow the blades to open and close in a gently lulling motion. The caption read:

SCISSORS AT THE WEDDING PARTY

One wishing ill to the bridegroom stands behind the happy man and, holding an open pair of scissors, calls his name. If the groom turns to answer the scissors are snapped shut whereupon the groom is rendered incapable of consummating the marriage.

And there were a good couple dozen other displays as well, each lovingly and meticulously rendered: uncertain and unsettling, and very funny—and then not.

As I was getting set to leave, I noticed a deliciously browned single-portion pie mounted alongside a burnt piece of toast. There were two dead mice on the toast. MOUSE CURES read the pieces' joint caption, although each

Mice on toast and mouse pie

of the dishes had its own legend as well. The caption under the first read: "Mouse Pie, when eaten with regularity, serves as a remedy for children who stammer." The label under the burnt toast read: "Bed wetting or general incontinence of urine can be controlled by eating mice on toast, fur and all."

After which, there followed an italicized citation:

A flayne Mouse, or made in powder and drunk at one tyme, doeth perfectly helpe such as cannot holde or keepe their water: especially, if it be used three days in this order. This is verie trye and often puruved.

1579 Lupton
Thousand Notable Things I / 40

Right then and there I made myself a promise; and I've kept it: I have not gone to the library to track down that Lupton reference. There has to be an end to all this.

No, really.

IT WAS GETTING LATE—in fact, this time I was late for a plane—so I bid David a quick goodbye, and let myself out through a passageway leading from the workroom into the museum proper. The space immediately on the other side of the workroom wall, which would soon be housing "Tell the Bees," was in the meantime filled with a wonderful traveling exhibition on loan from the Mütter

Museum. Now, I'd heard of the Mütter Museum, and I knew that it actually does exist. It was founded in 1858 when Dr. Thomas Dent Mütter presented his unique (and unquestionably bizarre) teaching collection of anatomical and pathological curiosa to the College of Physicians of Philadelphia, where it resides (having been steadily augmented) to this day. It's the sort of place where you can find the skeleton of a giant (7′6″) looming over the skeleton of a dwarf (3′6″), or the skeleton (skeletons?) of Siamese twins, or wax casts of all manner of malignancies, or the actual tumor removed from President Grover Cleveland's jaw during a secret operation in 1893.*

The Mütter's show at the Jurassic featured an array of arcane and vaguely threatening antique surgical instruments, the plaster cast of a trephined skull from Peru, various gallstones, some astonishing photographs of sliced heads and haunting (haunted) bell jars, wax models of syphilitic tongues . . . There was a heartrendingly luminous display, across a flat expanse of black

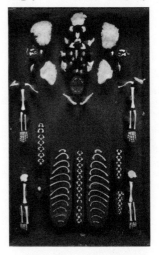

velvet, lovingly lit, of the 206 minute incipient bones extracted from a miscarried three-month fetus, each bone separated out and gleaming: the rib cage like a delicate array of filleted fishbones, the fingertips like so many flakes of stray dandruff.

Disarticulated skeleton of a three-month-old fetus from the Mütter Museum collection, Philadelphia

*Dr. Chevalier Jackson's drawer
of inhaled objects*

There was a teeming little chest of drawers, compiled by a punctilious physician named Chevalier Jackson during the early decades of this century, and containing, across a splay of neatly divided interior compartments, highlights from the collection of miscellaneous foreign bodies the good doctor had managed to extract over the years from the windpipes and digestive tracts of various choking victims (jacks, rings, chains, crucifixes, marbles, doll arms, a toy battleship), complete with documentation as to the age, identity, and fate of the various inhalers.

Everything was actual, everything was real, including . . .

It was getting very late now, and, really, I *had* to be going, but just as I was heading out the door I happened to gaze into one final display case, over to the side, and there, tellingly spotlit, lay the actual solitary remains of *a real human horn*, an incurled protrusion ("20 cm long and between 1 and 3 cm in diameter") sawed off the skull of an unnamed seventy-year-old woman in the middle of the last century by one S. Beaus, M.D.

So, go figure.*

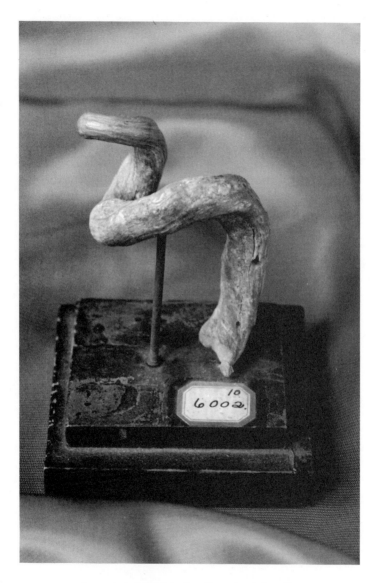

A woman's horn (nineteenth century) from the
Mütter Museum collection, Philadelphia

Notes

David Wilson: the director outside his museum

PART I: INHALING THE SPORE

p. 46: ". . . how she puts up with all this."
Diana's father, I learned in a subsequent conversation, came from Terre Haute, Indiana, though he died when she was still a young girl. David's own father hailed from Lincoln, Nebraska. His mother's family tapped back into Ireland, specifically to Ulster. Such details would emerge in our conversations from time to time—a mention of Socorro, New Mexico, with its vast array of radio telescopes deployed atop coursing railroad cars; or of Düsseldorf, the hometown of the artist and latter-day shaman Joseph Beuys—but always, and only, tangentially. Whenever I endeavored to get David to divulge the specific meanings behind the mysteriously evocative sequence of place names on the copyright pages of his various museum publications more directly, he'd turn

especially vague and elusive, squirming evasively and then blandly shifting the subject. Mal en Beg and Mal en Mor, it eventually turned out, are small villages in County Donegal, Ireland, on the republican side of the Ulster border. Bhopal, Beirut, Pretoria, Teheran? "Several places where a great deal of suffering was taking place at the time," David indicated mildly one morning before catching himself up short and quickly going all blank again.

p. 51: . . . who either was or wasn't Gerard Billius's granddaughter.

Wilson's exhalation of foggy indeterminacy, for that matter, often seems to insinuate itself into the world itself. I was able, somewhat later, to track down a Mary Rose Cannon in Pasadena, and she did indeed hail from Texas; she knew Wilson, and she had in fact contributed several early collections to the museum ("the butterflies, for instance"); she had, she told me, all sorts of other collections salted away in her garage (including bird feathers, rattlesnake paperweights, piranha paperweights, and old nineteenth-century glass chemists' beakers used in the manufacture of perfume); but when I asked her whether she was in fact the granddaughter of a lawyer named Gerard Billius, she grew quiet for a moment. "Well," she said at length, "could be. I mean, I was adopted, you see, so I never really knew my grandparents. In fact I came very near to being adopted by Roy Rogers and Dale Evans. They came to the orphanage, he dandled me on his knee, and they were just about set to take me, only it turned out that they wanted a girl alone and I came with my brother—we were a kind of package deal—and so they passed and we were eventually adopted by somebody else. They changed our name, and we never really knew our grandparents. Though we did get some stuff from them after they died."

p. 53: . . . "between" him and the world.

In particular, David wanted to make sure that I at very least credit the "absolutely invaluable contributions" of such museum colleagues as Mark Francis Rossi (Chief Keeper), Sarah Simons (Administrative Director/Librarian), Harold Chambers (Head of Research), Rex Ravenelle (Head of Exhibitions), Kristina Marrin (Curator), and Bridget Marrin (Curatorial Assistant).

p. 62: "The first layers are just a filter . . ."

I was momentarily reminded of Rainer Maria Rilke's epistolary advice to a young poet:

"Irony: Do not let yourself be governed by it, especially not in uncreative moments. In creative moments try to make use of it as one more means of grasping life. Cleanly used, it too is clean, and one need not be ashamed of it; and if you feel you are getting too familiar with it, if you fear this growing intimacy with it, then turn to great and serious objects, before which it becomes small and helpless. Seek the depth of things: thither irony never descends—and when you come thus close to the edge of greatness, test out at the same time whether this ironic attitude springs from a necessity of your nature. For under the influence of serious things either it will fall from you (if it is something fortuitous), or else it will (if it really innately belongs to you) strengthen into a stern instrument and take its place in the series of tools with which you will have to shape your art." (Rilke, *Letters to a Young Poet*; trans., M. D. Herter; New York: Norton, 1993; p. 24.)

PART II: CEREBRAL GROWTH

p. 74: . . . the secret society's *First Encyclopedia of Tlön.*

Borges's story is in fact immensely evocative of Wilson's project as well. "The metaphysicians of Tlön," Borges notes, "are not looking for truth, not even an approximation of it; they are after a kind of amazement." Elsewhere he records how "One of the schools of Tlön has reached the point of denying time. It reasons that the present is undefined, that the future has no other reality than as present hope, that the past is no more than present memory. Another school declares that the *whole of time* has already happened and that our life is a vague memory or dim reflection, doubtless false and fragmented, of an irrevocable process" (p. 25). Readers will of course have noted how the Iguazú Falls, where Geoffrey Sonnabend spent his long night of revelation in 1936, is just a few hundred miles north of Buenos Aires, where Borges was at the same time holding sway as a senior librarian. As for Wilson's own knowledge of the Borges story, he turned all coy on the subject when I asked him directly, though when I asked whether the "Buenos Aires" reference in his

The librarian of Buenos Aires

litany of place names on the copyright
page of the various museum publications in fact constituted an allusion to
Borges, the way "Düsseldorf" seems to
allude to Beuys, he smiled and did not contradict me.

As for this last bit of conjecture, however, one might
consider a passage from Volume 1, number 1 of Ricky
Jay's *Journal of Anomalies* (Los Angeles, spring 1994).
(Jay, incidentally, is also a fan of the MJT.) After describing a famous calculating-dog act from nineteenth-century
London, Jay notes how Charles Dickens himself somewhere records having attended this dog's performance
twice before going backstage to confront the dog's owner
with his own clever theory about how the man had gotten the dog to choose precisely the right card. "And he did
not deny my discovery of his principle," Dickens reports
smugly.

To which Jay adds: "This scenario has a surprisingly
modern ring, not in the performance of the dog but
rather in the interchange between the amateur and professional conjurer. In the time-honored tradition, the amateur, thoroughly fooled, returns to scrutinize the show.
He intuits a method which, although almost certainly in-
correct (or at best providing only a partial explanation),
satisfies him. He now confronts the conjurer (unlike
many of his present-day counterparts, Dickens had the
courtesy to wait for the room to clear) and proudly an-
nounces his theory. The performer smiles and says noth-

ing. This the amateur interprets as a sign of assent. Convinced of his remarkable powers of observation and
analysis, the tyro departs, basking in the glow of self-
congratulation."

p. 77: . . . phosphorescent by night.)
Or, to give another example, consider the testimony of
Edward Brown, from his 1673 monograph *A Brief Account of Some Travels in divers Parts of Europe* . . . (I'll
spare you the full title, which goes on for another whole
paragraph), who records that while in Leipzig he visited
the Burgomeister, one Herr von Adlershelme, "a courte-
ous Learned Person, and great virtuoso, who has col-
lected and observed many things," and who had gathered
together in his "Chamber of Rarities" many things that
were—the word Brown uses is: "considerable." Promising to confine his own list to "but a few," Brown then goes
on to enumerate:

> An Elephant's Head with the dentes molares in it. An
> Animal like an Armadillo, but the scales are much larger
> and the Tail broader. Very large flying Fishes. A Sea-
> horse. Bread of Mount Libanus. A Cedarbranch with the
> Fruit upon it. Large Granates as they grow in the Mine.
> A Siren's hand. A Chameleon. A piece of Iron, which
> seems to be the head of a Spear, found in the Tooth of an
> Elephant, the Tooth being grown about it. The Isle of
> Jersey drawn by our King Charles the Second. A piece of
> wood with the Blood of King Charles the First upon it.
> A Greenland Lance with a large Bell at the end of it.
> Much Japan painting, wherein their manner of hunting
> and working may be observed. A Picture of our Saviour
> [upon] the Hatches [of] which are . . . written . . . the

story of his Passion. Bevers taken in the River Elbe. A Picture of the murther of the Innocents, done by Albrecht Durer. Pictures of divers strange Fowls. A Greenland Boat. The skins of white Bears, Tigres, Wolves, and other Beasts. And I must not omit the Garter of an English Bride, with the story of it; of the Fashion in England for the Bridemen to take it off and wear it in their Hat, which seemed so strange to the Germans, that I was obliged to confirm it to them, by assuring them that I had divers times wore such a Garter my self.

A bloody piece of wood, a stuffed beaver, an elephant's tusk, a siren's hand, a bridal garter, *and a painting by Dürer*—not an untypical trove. Nor is it untypical for the provenance of many of what we today consider Renaissance and Baroque masterpieces to wend their way back through hodgepodge collections such as these.

p. 78: ". . . the whole body momentarily convulsed."
Of course the Americans whom the Europeans were suddenly encountering could have been, for their part, no less startled. In a journal entry describing one of his first landfalls, off the island of Tortuga on December 18, 1492, Columbus describes how a native "king" and several of his "counsellors" canoed out to his boat and participated in an exchange of gifts: "Many [of the] things that passed between them I did not understand," Columbus confesses, "except that I saw well that they took everything as a great wonder" (quoted in Greenblatt, *Marvelous Possessions;* Chicago: University of Chicago Press, 1991; p. 13). And even though such an estimation

may in part be laid to projection, still, the sense of awe can well be imagined—and *has* been, repeatedly, for instance in the first volume of the Uruguayan writer Eduardo Galeano's *Memory of Fire* trilogy (Vol. I: *Genesis;* trans., Cedric Belfrage; New York: Pantheon, 1985), wherein several such moments are rekindled. For example, when the Molucca Indians first saw the small landing craft being launched from Magellan's galleons, "they thought those boats were small daughters of the ships, that the ships gave them birth and suckled them" (pp. 73–74). Other natives elsewhere suddenly awoke, uncomprehending, barely believing, to the sight of whole floating islands with downy cloudbanks flapping in the breeze, newly bobbing off their shores. And the Aztecs famously took Cortés's men atop their horses for gods.

Curiously, this spirit of wonder—of the astonishment of the world—persisted much longer in Latin America than it did in the North (perhaps, in part, because the native peoples themselves persisted much longer, both as distinct races and through intermarriage). Surely this accounts in part for the continuing Latin American literary penchant for magic realism. Not for nothing is Borges an Argentinean. Or consider, in this context, the discovery of ice at the end of the first chapter of Gabriel García Márquez's *One Hundred Years of Solitude* (trans., Gregory Rabassa; New York: Harper & Row, 1970; p. 26):

> Little José Arcadio refused to touch it. Aureliano, on the other hand, took a step forward and put his hand on it, withdrawing it immediately. "It's boiling," he exclaimed,

startled. But his father paid no attention to him. Intoxicated by the evidence of the miracle, he forgot at that moment about the frustration of his delirious undertakings and Melquíades' body, abandoned to the appetite of the squids. He paid another five reales and with his hand on the cake, as if giving testimony on the holy scriptures, he exclaimed:

"This is the greatest invention of our time."

p. 78: ". . . my heart trembles."

"Once ashore, I ambled along the Avenida Rio Branco, where once the Tupinamba villages stood; in my pocket was that breviary of the anthropologist, Jean de Léry. He had arrived in Rio three hundred and seventy-eight years previously, almost to the day." Claude Lévi-Strauss, recalling his 1934 arrival in Rio in *Tristes Tropiques* (trans., John Russell; New York: Atheneum, 1961; p. 85). A few pages later, Lévi-Strauss refers to Léry's book as "that masterpiece of anthropological literature" (p. 88).

p. 79: ". . . emotional center of witness."

This line of speculation leads toward some of the most engrossing analysis in Greenblatt's book, for he goes on to ask about the *function* of all this marveling. Yes, Columbus was overwhelmed with all the wonder he was experiencing—the word itself recurs in his journals and dispatches so often that the King of Spain himself at one point suggested that Columbus should be called not *Almirante*, the admiral, but rather *Admirans*, the one who wonders (p. 83). But so much wonder was also a useful screen (I'm greatly oversimplifying Greenblatt's argument here) for in his writings "Columbus tries to draw

Admirans *(the one who wonders)*

the reader toward wonder, a
sense of the marvelous that in
effect fills up the emptiness at
the center of the maimed rite of
possession." Greenblatt is referring to that moment, repeated
time and again, when, following an exchange of trinkets,
Columbus claims title to the respective islands in the
name of the King of Spain, and none of the native in-
habitants contradict him, which he in turn takes for assent. "But that ritual had at its center . . . a defect, an
absurdity, a tragicomic invocation of the possibility of a
refusal that could not in fact possibly occur [if for no
other reason than that the two parties didn't even speak
each other's language, let alone comprehend each other's
conception of property, etc.]: *y no me fué contradicho*"
(p. 80).

In the years after Columbus, the European sensibility's virtual debauch in the wonder of the New World allowed it to disguise, from itself, the unprecedented
human decimation that was taking place over there, on
the ground, at that very moment. Wonder-besotted Europeans were so bedazzled that they could simply *fail to
notice* the carnage transpiring under their very eyes, in
their very name. We might say, to borrow Sartre's phrase,
that this continent was in bad faith.

In such matters it might also be wise to follow the
lead of Walter Benjamin—and if ever there was an in-

tellectual heir to the spirit of the *Wunderkammer* in our own time, it was he—who famously noted, in an essay reproduced in his *Illuminations* (trans., Harry Zohn; New York: Schocken, 1969) that "a historical materialist views [cultural treasures] with cautious detachment. For without exception the cultural treasures he surveys have an origin which he cannot contemplate without horror. . . . There is no document of civilization which is not at the same time a document of barbarism. And just as such a document is not free of barbarism, barbarism taints also the manner in which it is transmitted from one owner to another." This is the passage which culminates with his urging the student of culture "to brush history against the grain" (pp. 256–57).

p. 80: . . . the profusion of *Wunderkammern.*

And, of course, not just of *Wunderkammern:* European culture across the board was similarly besotted. John Donne, on "Going to Bed" with his mistress (his "Elegy 19," composed during the same 1590s as Platter's inventory of Cope's collection):

> License my roving hands, and let them go
> Before, behind, between, above, below.
> O my America! my new-found-land,
> My kingdom, safeliest when with one man manned,
> My mine of precious stones, my empery,
> How blest am I in discovering thee!

p. 81: . . . not quite so easily debunkable after all.

Two years ago my then five-year-old daughter Sara

fervently believed in Santa Claus. Last year she knew he was make-believe. But this year her belief in him was more passionate, and more ornately buttressed, than ever before.

p. 88: . . . must travel to St. Petersburg.

Rosamond Wolff Purcell did precisely that as part of her marvelous photographic collaboration with Stephen Jay Gould in their book *Finders, Keepers: Treasures and Oddities of Natural History* (New York: Norton, 1992). The first chapter concerns itself entirely with the remarkable relationship between Frederik Ruysch and Peter the Great. The two had in fact first met some twenty years before Peter purchased the collection when, as a teenager, the future tsar had been traveling through Europe, working incognito in shipyards in England and Holland, systematically amassing the hands-on experience he would soon be deploying in his headlong drive to modernize Russia. The purchase of Ruysch's emporium, in 1717, was part of a massive campaign on Peter's part to build up, from virtual scratch, one of the greatest *Wunderkammern* on the continent, an effort in which he was arguably successful, though he died not long after, in 1725. Ruysch outlived him by another six years. (See also Robert Massie's *Peter the Great: His Life and World*; New York: Knopf, 1980; pp. 187, 814.)

Simon Schama's book on Dutch culture of the Golden Age, *The Embarrassment of Riches* (New York: Knopf, 1987), includes a startling 1683 painting by Jan van Neck entitled *The Anatomy Lesson of Dr. Frederik Ruysch* in which "a dead infant is the object of the sur-

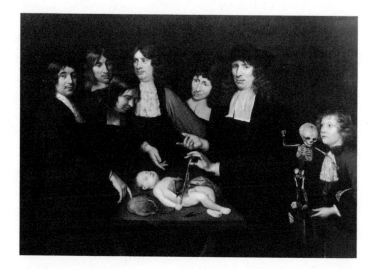

Jan van Neck, The Anatomy Lesson of
Dr. Frederik Ruysch *(1683)*

geon's dissection while the anatomist's own son, shown
at right, ponders simultaneously the mysteries of mortal
flesh and immortal science" (p. 526). That may be
Ruysch's son, but it could just as well have been his
daughter, Rachel, who also assisted her father from an
early age (not only attending his anatomical dissections
but also sewing the lace cuffs, for example, for some of
his most famous infant preparations) and who grew into
one of the foremost painters of her own age, a specialist
in exactingly observed still lifes, particularly floral
arrangements, which were enormously prized and even
outsold the works of Rembrandt. Her painting career
spanned seven decades; she died at age eighty-six, in
1750.

p. 89: . . . advances in positivist certainty.

There were, of course, exceptions—a counterflow to the undertow. The Ashmolean's Arthur MacGregor gives us the English polymath Henry Peacham complaining, as early as 1611, with regard to the sudden profusion of wonder-cabinets: "Why does the rude vulgar so hastily post in madnesse to gaze at trifles and toyes not worth viewing?" (*Tradescant's Rarities*, p. 17). By this time England was already teeming with enough private collections to attract, as MacGregor goes on, "the attention of less scrupulous dealers and the irony of the skeptical." He quotes the satirist Thomas Nashe as writing of these gullible magpies that "a thousand guegawes and toyes have they in their chambers, which they heape up together, with infinite expence, and are made beleeve of them that sell them, that they are rare and pretious thinges, when they have gathered them upon some dunghill" (p. 71). Shakespeare, in *The Tempest* (1611), has Trinculo salivating at the prospect of getting the savage Caliban back to England. He is certain he can bring the "holiday fools" out in force to pay for the opportunity to gawk at the monster. "When they will not give a doit to relieve a lame beggar, they will lay out ten to see a dead Indian" (II, ii, 30–32).

And for that matter, as we shall presently see, there were a spate of other objections, as well, grounded in the resurgent spirit of a regrouping positivist science. Galileo, for instance, had little use for those "curious little men" who could amuse themselves, like children, in collecting small and insignificant things, "a petrified crab, a desiccated chameleon, a fly or spider in gelatin or amber, those small clay figurines, supposedly found in ancient Egyptian burial chambers." His contempt extended to the whole hoarding sensibility, whatever its medium of expression: "Our poet errs as much as would a painter who, purposing to depict a particular hunting scene, were to clutter his canvas with conies, hares, foxes, goats, deer, wolves, bears, lions, tigers, boars, hounds, greyhounds, leopards, and all manner of wild beasts"—a list that sounds uncannily like the almond stone at the MJT—"clustering at will animals of the hunt with every sort of game such as to liken his painting more unto a representation of the entry into the Ark of Noah than unto a natural hunting scene." (quoted in Lugli, "Inquiry as Collection"; *Res*; autumn 1986; pp. 109–11).

And yet, withal . . . William Schupbach, after cataloguing a raft of similar such objections in his erudite contribution to the *Origins* volume, concludes that "Against these negative judgments must be set the actions of creators of cabinets such as Casabona, van Heurn, du-Molinet and Francke, whose desire for certain knowledge was not so consuming as to kill their appreciation of the old, the fragmentary, and the enigmatic" (p. 178).

p. 90: ". . . as the essence of knowing."

Or, in a similar vein, consider Albert Einstein: "The most beautiful experience we can have is the mysterious. It is the fundamental emotion which stands at the cradle of true art and true science. Whoever does not know it can no longer wonder, no longer marvel, is as good as dead, and his eyes are dimmed" (Einstein, *Ideas and Opinions*; New York: Crown, 1954; p. 11).

Incidentally, the name of Feynman's son Carl is to be found among those gracing the list of patrons of the Museum of Jurassic Technology.

p. 90: . . . premodern wellsprings of the postmodern temper.

In his book *Art & Discontent: Theory at the Millennium* (Kingston: McPherson & Co., 1991), the art critic Thomas McEvilley develops the notion of the periodic recurrence of the postmodern, or rather the theory that modernist and postmodernist tendencies have actually been following one upon the other throughout history. In this context, for example, he uncovers a striking set of affinities between our own postmodernist ethos and that of the Alexandrian/Hellenistic age (see pp. 98 ff.).

I suppose, in thinking about the MJT, we might similarly speak of the periodic recurrence of the *pre*modern. Or are the two types of recurrences (of the postmodern and the premodern) in fact the same thing? (One might note, in this context, the way in which so much of the premodern thought of the sixteenth and seventeenth centuries likewise derived, as we will presently be seeing, from hermetic and occult traditions first codified in the Alexandrian/Hellenistic and early Christian periods.)

p. 93: . . . drowned in her own pond.

The account of the affair by Martin Welch, included in the *Tradescant's Rarities* volume, goes to considerable lengths to cast Ashmole himself as the aggrieved party, with Hester supposedly being the one who behaved erratically and dishonorably. To hear Welch tell it (with almost overheated rhetorical intensity), any other version would "stretch our credulity to its limits."

p. 94: . . . for that wonder's domestication and standardization.)

Astrology, alchemy, witchcraft trials, the occult, and the hermetic in general . . . The appearance of Mr. Ashmole in our brief survey highlights another source, besides the discovery of the New World, feeding the wonder sensibility that animated so much of the intellectual life of the sixteenth and seventeenth centuries, and particularly its profusion of wonder-cabinets. The awakening of wonder also drew on a recovery, as it were, of the Old World, and in particular the resurrection of various Alexandrine/Hellenistic and early Christian doctrines regarding the nature of the universe and the human capacity for free agency within that universe that had been banished as rabidly heretical ever since the time of Augustine. Frances Yates famously traced the sixteenth-century upwelling of such long-suppressed motifs in her seminal *Giordano Bruno and the Hermetic Tradition* (University of Chicago Press, 1964). In particular she analyzed the impact upon all sorts of humanist masters during this period of the rediscovery of the so-called *Corpus Hermeticum*, a second-century-A.D. compendium of treatises codifying several convergent strains of Neoplatonist and Gnostic numerological and astral magics that these sixteenth-century masters initially mistook to be the work of a single, primordial Egyptian magus, a contemporary of Abraham's, named Hermes Trismegistus (or Hermes the Thrice-Great), who in turn was in some mysterious way identified with the Greek god Hermes himself. It's easy to see how such humanists as Giordano Bruno would have been drawn to a set of doctrines that seemed to predate all the religious schisms that had in the meantime so bloodily erupted everywhere around them. (For refusing to renounce his allegiance to such open-ended investigations, Bruno was himself burned at the stake in 1600.)

And then, of course, there was the parallel resurgence, during this same period and among many of the same people, of interest in the twinned disciplines of astrology and alchemy. The first chapter in William Brock's recent *Norton History of Chemistry* (New York: Norton, 1992) is entitled "On the Nature of the Universe and the Hermetic Museum." (Not coincidentally, one of the main elements deployed in alchemical practice, quicksilver, had since late Hellenistic times been known as Mercury—the Roman name for the Greek god Hermes, and the same name astrologers had affixed to the planet at a similarly early date.) In fact, chemistry as we now know it gradually began to emerge from out of the strange obsessive labors of the alchemical magi.

Time and again, students of seventeenth-century intellectual history (who have to be having some of the most fun of anyone in Academe) find themselves wending their way back into this strange material (their entire field is one vast cabinet of curiosities). Allison Coudert, for example, recounts the story of Francis Mercury van Helmont (1614–1698), whose father, the Belgian Jan Baptista van Helmont, was one of the most significant figures in the early history of modern chemistry (he rates five full pages in Brock's book). The son's birth "occurred shortly after his father, a very good chemist and not one to be easily fooled, claims to have transmuted eight ounces of base metal into gold. This unusual event may explain the infant's unusual name, Mercury, redolent as it was with alchemical associations." (See Coudert's essay in *The Shapes of Knowledge from the Renaissance to the Enlightenment* [ed. Ronald R. Kelley and Richard H. Popkin; Deventer, Netherlands: Kluwer Academic Publishers, 1991; p. 84].) Mercury van Helmont in turn grew into one of the foremost Christian popularizers of such Hebrew Kabbalistic texts as the Zohar. He also happened to be close friends with Gottfried Leibniz (1646–1716), and Coudert makes a strong case for the Kabbalistic roots of both Leibniz's monadology and his calculus (his explorations, that is, of the infinite and the infinitesimal).

In a similar vein, John Maynard Keynes, of all people, startled a Cambridge audience in 1946 with his contention that "Newton [1642–1727] was not the first of the age of reason. He was the last of the magicians, the last of the Babylonians and Sumerians, the last great mind which looked out on the visible and intellectual

world with the same eyes as those who began to build our intellectual inheritance less than 10,000 years ago." Keynes went on to note how, in terms of alchemy and other such esoteric practices, during the first

The alchemist of Cambridge

phase of his intellectual life, "Newton was clearly an un-
bridled addict," and this "during the very years when he
was composing the *Principia!*" Keynes, who had examined
hundreds of pages of Newton's own records on his esoteric investigations (preserved in the Cambridge archives),
concluded: "It is utterly impossible to deny that [they
are] wholly magical and wholly devoid of scientific value;
and also impossible not to admit that Newton devoted
years of work to [them]" (from "Newton, the Man" in
Keynes, *Essays in Biography* [New York: Norton, 1963; pp.
311, 318–19]). Of course, in his later years Newton left
such divagations behind, turning to posterity the rigor-
ously scientific face by which he is so much better known;
he never allowed those alchemical papers to be published
or even reviewed during his lifetime. But nor did he ever
order them destroyed.

All of these various arcane doctrines and practices
shared certain premises of relevance to the *Wunderkam-*
mer sensibility, to begin with an innate (and distinctly
new—or, anyway, renewed) belief in the fundamental
perfectibility of man, his ability to transcend Adam's
fallen destiny on his own (without necessarily having to
rely on Christ's intervention), or at any rate the ability of
the individual initiate, the particular magus, to do so. Yes,
to be sure, the alchemist, for instance, was trying to
transmute base metals into gold, but this was always seen
as occurring in tandem with, and metaphorical of, trans-
formations he was attempting to enact on his own person.
In working on these material elements, he was working
on the spiritual elements within himself as well, work
that in turn might eventually have stupendous implica-

tions for the world at large. (Think of David Wilson's own experience of revelation and mission in this context.) All of these labors transpired within the context of a Neoplatonist view of the universe (in Coudert's characterization) "as a great chain of being in which planets, men, animals, vegetables, minerals, and metals are linked together in complex hierarchies of correspondences," a view which "encouraged the belief that every existing thing is in some measure a symbol, or reflection, of something else," with each of them in turn containing to some degree an emanation of the divine unity which overarched them all (p. 92).

Hence the impulse to collect and catalogue and explore everything—and hence the proliferation of interest in wonder-cabinets. Kircher, for instance, took to filling his Jesuit Museum in Rome with examples of Egyptian hieroglyphs, convinced that they had been invented by Hermes Trismegistus himself and feverishly intent on cracking their secret code (see Yates, p. 417). As for Ashmole, Yates convincingly suggests that his own intellectual genealogy wends back to Bruno's visit to Oxford in 1583–84, during which this "Hermetic magician of the most extreme type" preached his new philosophy, grounded in its Egyptian revelation. Some two generations later, she goes on to note, Ashmole became England's "first known Freemason" (p. 415) and as such a secret initiate in a similar set of supposedly Egyptian-derived mysteries.

p. 95: . . . things that were "strang."
In addition, such letters testify to a wealth of human

The cabinetman of Copenhagen

responses—notable among them, petulant envy—that, alas, are far from strange. When the Danish cabinetman Ole Worm's son, Willum, visited the Ark in 1658 and subsequently wrote his father to tell him about the experience, Ole wrote back, concerning Tradescant the Elder, "I have heard that he was an Idiot." (Quoted in *Tradescant's Rarities*, p. 21, n. 17.)

p. 97: . . . any stray pilgrims from the Jurassic.
Nor were these unique instances of such microminiaturist art. In fact, it turns out there was a veritable craze for the microminiature during the sixteenth century, so much so that many of the *Wunderkammer* cognoscenti of our own day, such as several of the contributors to the *Origins* volume, are given to ho-humming the occasional "obligatory cherry stone" they're forced to include among their own various inventories (p. 154).

The Tradescants' collection alone included such other feats as "a nest of 52 wooden cups turned within each other as thin as paper," a cherrystone containing a dozen wooden spoons and another inscribed with the faces of "88 emperors," and a "Halfe a Hasle-nut with 70 pieces of householdstuffe in it" (*Tradescant's Rarities*, p. 93).

In part, this fascination was but a microminiature rendition of the *Wunderkammer* passion itself—the world in a cabinet as recalibrated in terms of the roomful in a nutshell. Such an analogy was rendered virtually explicit on the Tradescants' own family tombstone, upon which a poet celebrated, *inter alia,*

> Whilst they (as Homer's Iliad in a nut)
> A world of wonders in one cabinet shut.
>
> (*Tradescant's Rarities*, p. 15)

But the taste for microminiaturism was as much a celebration of the sudden advances in the new technologies, both of the lathe and the lens, that made such efforts possible (technological advances just as portentous as those that were suddenly allowing the circumnavigation of the globe), as it was of any individual craftsman's specific virtuosity. In Dresden, according to MacGregor, the lathes, tools, and magnifying glasses were every bit as venerated as the objects they produced (including, for instance, one cherrystone carved with *180* faces!) and were frequently exhibited right alongside those objects on their own elaborate mounts (*Tradescant's Rarities*, p. 75).

Settala, in Milan, faced a problem which we in turn have faced in the production of this book, for, according to Adalgisa Lugli, he complained in the manuscript catalogues to his own collection about "finding it impossible to adequately portray through illustration the 'minutiae'—such items as an ivory cherrystone enclosing in its pit a full complement of chess pieces, ever-fine strands of ivory, a camel that passes through the eye of a needle, or a loom on which to weave a spider's web, all of which he himself fashioned at the lathe" (Lugli, p. 119).

The problem of reproducing microminiature details
has also lately been confounding computer technologists
who've been trying to digitalize the contents of major
art museums. According to a recent article by Phil Pat-
ton in the *New York Times* (August 7, 1994), technicians
at the National Gallery in Washington have been having
a particularly difficult time scanning the fifteenth-
century Flemish master Rogier van der Weyden's painting *St. George and the Dragon* into their computer files:
"On the painting's background, behind the knight and
the monster, is a walled city. So finely rendered is the detailed landscape that [when scanned,] the image
'dithered,' or began to 'pixilate' into a gridlike pattern
not unlike what one would expect if a snapshot were
taken through a screen door. . . . The dithering of 'St.
George' lent new meaning to an inscription in rather
shaky Latin on the back of the painting: Videatur et pon-
deretur. Ab arte reperitis. (Look and ponder. One dis-
covers things from art.) Seen close up, through a
photomicrograph, the background of the picture shows
street scenes in the walled city, people passing on the
streets, even an open window on whose sill sits a microscopic waterjug—all virtually as invisible to the human
eye as to the scanners. Trying to put 'St. George' on the
computer inspired wonder at how the painting was done
in the first place. With a single-hair brush, under a magnifying glass? 'That detail was there all along,' said Ms.
Vicki Porter, the computerized Visitor Center's director,
'just waiting to be discovered.' "

Of all the microminiaturist feats I came upon during
my own mock-scholarly dalliances, perhaps my own fa-

vorites were a pair I stumbled upon in a footnote in
Tradescant's Rarities, to wit: the achievements of a London smith named Mark Scaliot who, in 1578, produced "a
lock, of iron, steel and brass, of eleven several pieces, and
a pipe key, all of which weighed but one grain of gold. He
also made a chain of gold, of forty-three links, which
chain being fastened to the lock and key, and put about a
Flea's neck, the Flea drew with ease. Chain, key, lock, and
flea weighed but one grain and a half" (p. 94, n. 199).

p. 107: . . . secret operation in 1893.

The Mütter Museum recently earned the top ranking on
a "one-of-a-kind museums" list compiled by Weissman
Travel Reports, an information service for travel agents
(according to an item in the February 12, 1995, *Philadelphia Inquirer*). Runners-up, in descending order, included
the Barbie Museum in Palo Alto, California; the International Friendship Exhibition in Myoyangsan, North
Korea (gifts to the country's leaders); the Museum of
Two-Headed Animals, Bamberg, Germany; the City Museum, Iquitos, Peru (decaying bodies); the U.S.–Chiang
Kai-shek Criminal Acts Exhibition Hall, Chongqing,
China; and the Museum of the Inquisition, Lima, Peru.
The Museum of Menstruation in New Carrollton, Mary-
land, just missed making the list. The compilers of the
list appeared never to have heard of the Museum of
Jurassic Technology.

It was probably fitting that Mütter's collection found
a home in Philadelphia, the very city in which Charles
Willson Peale had opened his own museum back in 1786.
For that matter, both collections remind us how, even as

the *Wunder* sensibility faced decided opposition during its own period of hegemony, so it has managed to persist (if in somewhat attenuated form) through the centuries since its seeming overthrow by its more positivist rival.

In fact, the first half of the nineteenth century saw its own small resurgence of the *Wunder* sensibility, in part for the very same reasons as had pertained in the early sixteenth century, a suddenly expanded exposure, that is, to an entirely new world—in this instance, to China itself, which was suddenly experiencing a marked increase in Western penetration. In this context, Gretchen Worden, the director of the Mütter, alerted me to the existence of a marvelous unsigned item in the May 21, 1845, issue of the *Boston Medical and Surgical Journal* (Vol. 32, no. 16). "Our friends from the country who visit Boston on the coming anniversary must not forget to look in at the room in the Society for Medical Improvement," advises our anonymous would-be host (who Worden is convinced was none other than Dr. Oliver Wendell Holmes), for "a new accession has lately been made to its treasures which they will examine with greatest interest"—namely, a series of twenty-eight oil paintings "representing a great variety of cases of surgical disease, principally tumors, observed at the hospital at Canton under the care of Dr. Parker." As illustrations of disease, these paintings "are in the highest degree curious and instructive, and as works of art they may challenge the admiration of artists themselves. The gratitude of the Society for this very handsome gift would have naturally led to a wish that the portrait of the donor might have accompanied the other paintings—but it might have been unpleasant to our liberal friend to have been hung up on a wall as a *pendant* to a spina ventosa, or a *vis-à-vis* to fungus hæmatodes.

"These monstrous diseased growths are very serious things to our fellow-creatures of the Celestial empire," our suddenly circumspect tour guide acknowledges. "But they are so out of all reasonable proportions, and sprout up in such strange shapes and places—and China is so far off, and a China man is so much an abstraction to our minds—and the almond-shaped eyes, the pigtail, the brown-sherry complexion and the Oriental environments of the sufferers, so blind us to the naked fact of the existence of an unsightly or devouring malady, that we cannot help looking at them with a little twitching about the *levator anguli oris*, which if not inhuman is at least highly unbecoming."

Our contributor, however, immediately endeavors to wipe that unseemly smirk off his face, noting sagely that "The truth is, the practised eye kindles at the sight of any *very* remarkable excrescence, as the traveller's does at that of lofty mountains or colossal edifices." He goes on to note that one must journey to precisely such places as China—only just recently, and barely, touched by modern Western medical practices—if one is going to be able to witness them at all: "The pathological sublime and beautiful is so tamed down by the science of highly civilized countries, that the grander and more captivating efforts of nature in that department must be looked for among ruder people. We [in the West] nip the most promising growths of disease in the bud. Morbid products stand no better chance among the surgeons than apples in a

schoolhouse yard; they are all picked off long before they
are ripe. . . .

    "Not so in the pathological Eden of the Flowery Land:

> Nature here
> Wantons as in her prime, and plays at will
> Her virgin fancies.

"The first opening of the Chinese Hospital," our guide
continues, "was to the worshipper of morbid nature what
penetrating a Brazilian forest was to the botanist who
first explored its depths. The enormities of Asiatic hy-
pertrophy put his most extravagant steatomas and osteo-
sarcomas to the blush." And so forth, at considerably
greater and more florid length.

    Finally our host urges that "friends who dine with us,
and are always in such a hurry for the afternoon cars,
must not forget to see these pictures and the cabinet.
They had better give up the nuts and raisins than not to
see them. Indeed, if the question were between giving up
the pictures or the pudding itself, we would sacrifice the
latter—unless of a higher order than we have a right to
expect it to be."

p. 108: So, go figure.
And I did.

    It turns out that human horns, anomalous growths
consisting entirely of concentric layers of keratinized
epidermal cells with a tendency to originate on the sites
of sebaceous cysts, warts, or scars, are "far more frequent
than ordinarily supposed," according to Drs. George
Gould and Walter Pyle (*Anomalies and Curiosities of Med-*

icine; New York: Julian Press, 1956; p. 222). They can arise anywhere on the body, growing at a fairly slow but steady rate and often curling in on themselves, though generally nowadays they tend to get removed in the course of standard dermatological practice before they ever achieve any recognizable form as horns. And, in fact, they aren't exactly horns: they share the keratinized gloss and surface of standard animal horns, but they lack the bony core. Notwithstanding which, they have exerted a wondrous fascination on humankind, across cultures and centuries.

Drs. Gould and Pyle cite the 1820 case of a "Paul Rodrigues, a Mexican porter, who from the upper and lateral part of his head, had a horn 14 centimeters in circumference and divided into three shafts, which he concealed by constantly wearing a peculiarly shaped red cap" (p. 223). This cap-wearing strategy, however, doesn't always work: Martin Monestier (*Human Oddities*; Secaucus, N.J.: Citadel, 1978) cites the case of "a French peasant brought before a regional magistrate on September 18, 1598, for refusing to remove his hat in the presence of a nobleman. Forced to do so in court, he uncovered a well-developed ram's horn which, he explained, had begun to grow when he was five. The magistrate packed him off to see the king, who, according to one chronicler, 'sought to breed him with the courtesans.'" After a few months of this life, the poor fellow unfortunately gave up the ghost. On the other hand, Monestier also cites the example of François Trouillu, who was quite proud of his horn, "which closely resembled a panache."

Perhaps the most famous case in the early nineteenth century was that of the Parisian Madame Dimanche, "the

François Trouillu

The Widow Sunday

Widow Sunday," whose horn grew outward from her forehead and then down ten inches past her nose, almost to her chin. According to Monestier, "one day, at the age of 84, she suddenly decided to have it cut off. She knew her end was near and did not wish to meet her Maker wearing what she had begun to consider a Satanic ornament" (p. 111). She survived the operation of removal (by the famed Dr. Souberbeille) and lived another seven years. Mütter himself included a spooky wax cast of Madame Dimanche's face and horn among his collections, although there is some indication that several versions of the cast were in relatively common circulation at the time.

As for Mary Davis's allegedly lost horn, leave it to the indefatigable Arthur MacGregor, assistant keeper at the Ashmolean, to have tracked down every conceivable reference (see his piece in *The Ashmolean;* no. 3, 1983; pp. 10–11): a horn did indeed exist, in fact several. The Cheshire midwife cast off several pair, each set larger than the ones before ("in shew and substance much like a ram's horns," according to a contemporary pamphlet, "solid and wrinkled, but sadly grieving the old woman, especially upon the change of weather"). One of her horns was presented to the King of France "for the greatest rarity in nature, and was received with no less admiration." Her portrait was painted at least twice in 1668, when her age was given as seventy-four. One of those portraits went to the Ashmolean but was also lost (it appears, however, to have formed the basis for a surviving engraving). "From a historical point of view the disappearance of any part of the Museum's earliest collections is always to be regretted," MacGregor consoles himself, "but it has to be admitted that the loss of some is easier to bear than others. I for one can summon only the

Mary Davis of Saughall (1668)

mildest regret at being denied the opportunity of first-hand contact with Mary Davis's horn." (And, in fact, he may now be spared even that mild regret, since the horn appears in the meantime to have surfaced in Culver City, California.)

"Many ancient peoples believed that strength and fertility were concentrated in horns," Monestier points out, "hence the numerous cults worshipping bulls and rams. . . . Jupiter, the supreme Roman god, was depicted with horns, as was Isis, the Egyptian goddess of fertility. When Alexander the Great declared himself the son of Jupiter [or, actually, of Zeus], he ordered that all coins bearing his likeness should henceforth show him with horns. Moses was sometimes depicted with horns, as was Christ Himself. Many rulers had horns affixed to their helmets, as a symbol of power" (p. 110).

Monestier suggests that the association of horns with adultery and cuckoldry dates to Roman times, but in fact a primordial sense of the interrelationship between horns and sexuality—an understanding of the "horny," as it were—is embedded deep in the linguistic roots of our civilization. The master text in this regard is R. B. Onians's seminal, and in fact mind-boggling, *The Origins of European Thought about the Body, the Mind, the Soul, the World, Time and Fate* (Cambridge University Press, 1951). Norman O. Brown draws heavily on Onians's work, as for instance in this passage from *Love's Body* (New York: Random House, 1966):

> In the unconscious, cerebral is genital. The word *cerebral* is from the same root as Ceres, goddess of cereals, of

growth and fertility; the same root as *cresco*, to grow, and *creo*, to create. Onians, archaeologist of language, who uncovers lost worlds of meaning, buried meanings, has dug up a prehistoric image of the body, according to which head and genital intercommunicate via the spinal column: the gray matter of the brain, the spinal marrow, and the seminal fluid are all one identical substance, on tap in the genital and stored in the head. The soul-substance is the seminal substance: the genius is the genital in the head. (pp. 136–37)

By this reading, Freud's entire theory of sublimation is merely an unpacking of the possibilities already latent in the language itself. But it goes further than that, as Brown himself brought out in his most recent book, *Apocalypse and/or Metamorphosis* (University of California Press, 1991), for

English *horn* is Latin *cornu*, therefore English *corn*. Greek *keras* ("horn") is English *kern* and *kernel*; also . . . *Cornucopia*, horn of plenty.

But also *cornu* ("horn") is *corona* ("crown"). . . . And Greek *keras* ("horn") is Greek *kras*, English *cranium*, a head. Greek *kratos*, a head of power, an authority (aristocracy, demo-cracy); *krainein*, "authorize."

Herne the horny hunter [Falstaff's name in *The Merry Wives of Windsor* when he cavorts in the forest, horns on his brow] is German *Hirn* ("brain"). Herne was brainy; like the horned Moses, crescent, cresting. . . . A swollen or horny head; insane. *Cerebrosus (cerritus)*, which ought to mean "brainy," means "mad." Greek *keras* and *keraunos*, "horn" and "thunder," horn-mad and thunderstruck. (p. 38)

This latter passage is taken from Brown's essay on Actaeon, who turns out to be an enormously important figure in the Elizabethan imagination (as in the wider universe of wonder). The Elizabethans got their Actaeon from Ovid, more specifically from Arthur Golding's 1567 translation of the *Metamorphoses* (a text Ezra Pound once praised as "the most beautiful book in the language"). In Golding's rendition, Actaeon was out hunting in the forest with his hounds when he happened to catch a glimpse of Artemis/Diana (whom Golding also calls Phebe), the beautiful virgin goddess of the moon and of the hunt, bathing in a pool with her nymphs. Drawn by the extraordinary vision, Actaeon approaches silently, stealthily pulling aside the intervening branches—but he is seen:

> The Damsels at the sight of man quite out of count-
> nance dasht
> (Bicause they everichone were bare and naked to the
> quicke)
> (Book III, ll. 208–9)

But Phebe ("of personage so comly and so tall / That by the middle of hir necke she overpeered them all") stands her ground, fiercely defiant:

> though she had hir gard
> Of Nymphes about hir: yet she turnde hir bodie from
> him ward.
> And casting back an angrie looke, like as she would
> have sent
> An arrow at him had she had hir bow there readie bent,
> So raught she water in hir hande and for to wreake the
> spight

Besprinckled all the heade and face of this unluckie
knight, . . .
(ll. 220–25)

At which point his fate is already sealed:

[She] thus forespake the heavie lot that should upon
him light:
Now make thy vaunt among thy Mates, thou sawsts
Diana bare.
Tell if thou can: I give thee leave: tell hardily: doe not
spare.
This done she makes no further threates, but by and by
doth spread
A payre of lively olde Harts hornes upon his sprinckled
head.
(ll. 226–30)

As yet unknowing, Actaeon scampers off—"trottes," in
Golding's beguiling parlance—and it's only when he
comes upon a brook and gazes upon his own reflection in
the water . . .

when he saw his face
And horned temples in the brooke, he would have cryde
Alas,
But as for then no kinde of speach out of his lippes
could passe.
He sighde and brayde: for that was then the speach that
did remaine,
And downe the eyes that were not his, his bitter teares
did raine.
(ll. 236–40)

Within moments his own hounds have caught the scent of him and he is soon being pursued to his death.

Of course, in our context, we will understand the story of Actaeon's fate for what it is—a wonder narrative and a cautionary tale. (Fifteen years before his martyrdom, Giordano Bruno made repeated references to the Actaeon myth in his sequence of allegorical love poems, *De gli Eroici Furori*, published in England in 1585 and dedicated to Sir Philip Sidney. See Yates, pp. 275–84.) A story of possession: *Watch out for what you see.* (No sooner had Ovid himself completed his *Metamorphoses*, in A.D. 8, than he himself appears to have inadvertently witnessed something untoward—something sexual? something political? he doesn't say and we will never know—a calamitous misprision for which the great Augustus Caesar condemned him to eke out the remainder of his days in terrible exile along the farthest reaches of the Empire. "O why did I see what I saw?" the poet would be decrying his uncanny fate, a few years later, in Book II of his *Tristia.* "Actaeon never intended to see Diana naked / but still was torn to bits by his own hounds.") Antlers: from the French *antoeil* ("in the place of eyes") or the German *Augensprosse* ("eye-sprouts"). And recall, in this context, both the alchemical and the astrological symbols for Mercury, still in use today in both chemistry and astronomy: ☿.

When Chaucer's friend John Gower sang his version of the story, in his *Confessio Amantis* (also based on Ovid, though two hundred years before Golding), he cast Actaeon's fate as "an ensample touchende of mislok"—a truly wonderful three-way pun, for, of course, Actaeon had the bad luck to mislook upon Lady Luck. As might anyone risk to do, gazing too long, too helplessly, at Wonder. Not that it wouldn't necessarily be worth it.

Just ask the ant.

> *To my astonishment they take me home rather than to some secret hideaway and lock me in the catoptric room I had so carefully reconstructed from Athanasius Kircher's drawings. The mirrored walls return my image an infinite number of times. Had I been kidnapped by myself?*
>
> —ITALO CALVINO
> *If on a Winter's Night a Traveler*

Acknowledgments and Sources

The world will not perish for want of wonders,
but for want of wonder.
—J. B. S. HALDANE
(the geneticist mathematician)

This book would of course have been impossible without the always gracious (if continually wary) cooperation of its main subject, David Wilson. His sweet forbearance was all the more touching in light of his obvious underlying trepidations—as was true, for that matter, of his splendid wife, Diana, as well. (I have tried to keep faith with both of them.) Their daughter, Dan-Rae, showed no trepidations whatsoever and was an unmitigated delight throughout.

Along the way, as I myself was increasingly drawn into their museum's fascinational field, I was abetted by some wonderful fellow travelers—particularly John Walsh of the Getty Museum and Tom Eisner at Cornell. Ralph Rugoff, Rosamond Purcell, Ricky Jay, Allison Coudert, and Norman O. Brown were also improbably generous with their time and insights. Loisann Dowd

White at the Getty Center's library in Santa Monica; Gretchen Worden of the Mütter Museum in Philadelphia and Laura Lindgren, founder of the Museum's awesome annual calendar; Russell Lewis of the Chicago Historical Society; Beauvais Lyons and perhaps Vera Octavia of the Hokes Archives in Tennessee; William Willers and Walter Hamady of Wisconsin; Michael Fehr of the Karl Ernst Osthaus-Museum in Hagen, Germany (where a European outpost of the MJT has recently opened); and Arthur MacGregor and Oliver Impey of the Ashmolean Museum in Oxford were all indefatigably indulgent and marvelously helpful, as were Robin Palanker, Susie Einstein, and Piotr Bikont.

Lewis Lapham, Ilena Silverman, and Ben Metcalf at *Harper's* magazine sheltered an early version of this project when no one else could quite make heads or tails of it. Dan Frank at Pantheon then apparently saw something there and seemed to have a good time prodding it into book form, as did the book's unflappable designer, Kristen Bearse (or, anyway, I had a good time being thus prodded). My agent, Deborah Karl, both "got it" and stuck with it.

Finally, yet again, there's my own wondrous consort, Joasia. As David says of Diana—only more so—I really don't know how she puts up with all of this. But, as ever, and more and more, I cherish her for doing so.

As for more conventionally citable sources:

PART I: INHALING THE SPORE

The information on the Cameroonian stink ant, the *deprong mori* and the *Myotis lucifugus* bat, and Geoffrey Sonnabend and Madalena Delani all derive from exhibits at the Museum of Jurassic Technology in Los Angeles, California (9341 Venice Blvd., Culver City, CA 90212). The Society for the Diffusion of Useful Information, in conjunction with the Visitors to the Museum, has published two useful monographs: *Geoffrey Sonnabend: Obliscence: Theories of Forgetting and the Problem of Matter* (1991), an "encapsulation" by Valentine Worth with diagrammatic illustrations by Sona Dora; and *Bernard Maston, Donald Griffith and the Deprong Mori of the Tripsicum Plateau* (1964[*sic*]), also by Worth and Dora; both monographs are available from the museum. The Society and the Visitors have also published a booklet entitled *No One May Ever Have the Same Knowledge Again: Letters to Mount Wilson Observatory (1915–1935)* (1993), edited and transcribed by Sarah Simons (with complete photoreproductions of the letters themselves); this volume is likewise available from the museum, as is the pamphlet "The Museum of Jurassic Technology—and You," which features a full transcript of the museum's introductory audiovisual slide presentation. The early history of the Thums is detailed in a monograph entitled *On the Foundations of the Museum: The Thums, Gardeners and Botanists* (1993), by Illera Edoh, Keeper of the Foundation Collections—the first in what is slated to be a series of such "Foundations" monographs, available, again, through the MJT.

Donald Griffin's *Listening in the Dark: The Acoustic Orientation of Bats and Men* was published by the Yale University Press in 1958. Clement Silvestro's account of Charles Gunther's exploits, "The Candy Man's Mixed Bag," appeared in the fall 1972 issue (Vol. 2, no. 2) of *Chicago History* magazine. For more on Richard Whitten's Joyas del Trópico Húmedo museum, see Cathryn Domrose's article "A Romantic Evening with the Anthropods" in the *Tico Times* (San José, Costa Rica) of July 23, 1993.

Ralph Rugoff's lecture on the Museum of Jurassic Technology, "Beyond Belief: Museum as Metaphor," was delivered at the Dia Center for the Arts in New York City at a May 1993 symposium on *Visual Display: Culture Beyond Appearances*, all of the papers from which are being published, under that title, by the Seattle Bay Press (1995). Other accounts of the museum include: Maria Porges's "A Fictional Museum of Imaginary Truths" (*Artweek*, October 14, 1989); David Wharton's "Weird Science" (*Los Angeles Times*, December 13, 1989); and Frederick Rose's "Next Thing You Know, They'll Show Us a Slithy Tove" (*Wall Street Journal*, July 19, 1989).

The film *Stasis*, along with other film work by David Wilson, can be tracked down by way of Mr. Wilson himself, care of the museum.

Hagop Sandaldjian's microminiature oeuvre is slated to be the subject of a forthcoming museum publication, *Through the Eye of the Needle: The Unique World of Microminiatures of Hagop Sandaldjian*, with an introductory essay by Ralph Rugoff. (Other articles on Mr. Sandaldjian include: Alan Burdick's "Pope by a Hair" in the September 19, 1993, *New York Times Magazine;* and Lynn Andreoli Woods's "The Microminiaturist's Art between Heartbeats" in the December 28, 1990, *L.A. Reader*). Photographs from the MJT's Nanotechnology show were included in an article in the spring 1995 issue of *Felix.*

The photograph of *Camponotus floridanus* with his forehead rampant is courtesy of Tom and Maria Eisner.

PART II: CEREBRAL GROWTH

The centaur excavations at Volos, as rendered by William Willers of the University of Wisconsin at Oshkosh, were featured in a piece entitled "Do You Believe in Centaurs?" by Don Williams in the October 11, 1994, issue of the *Knoxville News Sentinel* on the occasion of the centaur exhibit at the University of Tennessee (which has in the meantime procured the exhibit for its permanent collection).

Donald Evans's imaginary philately was documented in Willy Eisenhart's *The World of Donald Evans* (New York: Abbeville, 1980, 1994). Charles Simonds's work has been the subject of numerous retrospectives (see, for instance, the catalogue to his 1982 show at the Museum of Contemporary Art in Chicago). Norman Daly's groundbreaking efforts were documented, many years after the fact, in *"The Civilization of Llhuros:* The First Multimedia Exhibition in the Genre of Archeological Fiction," by Mr. Daly himself with Beauvais Lyons, in *Leonardo* magazine, Vol. 24, no. 3, 1991 (London: Pergamon Press). (For an entertaining variant, consider David Macaulay's wittily turned and exquisitely illustrated *Motel of the Mysteries* [Boston: Houghton Mifflin, 1979], in which Howard Carson, an amateur archeologist in the year 4022, excavates the long-buried remains of an edifice dating back to the ancient civilization of Usa, a tacky motel which he proceeds to entirely misconstrue as a solemn place of worship.)

The Hokes Archives at the University of Tennessee in Knoxville (Beauvais Lyons, director; Vera Octavia, assistant director) have been the subject of numerous pamphlets and articles, including Vol. XII, no. 3 of the Cheekwood Fine Arts Center Monographs Series (Nashville, Tenn., spring 1990); Mr. Lyons's "The Excavation of the Apasht: Artifacts from an Imaginary Past" (*Leonardo* magazine, Vol. 18, no. 2, 1985); and a chapter in Linda Hutcheon's recent book *Irony's Edge: The Theory and Practice of Irony* (London and New York: Routledge, 1994).

Jorge Luis Borges's 1941 story "Tlön, Uqbar, Orbis Tertius" appeared in his 1956 volume *Ficciones* (English translation by Alastair Reid in the 1962 Grove Press edition).

The Origins of Museums: The Cabinet of Curiosities in Sixteenth- and Seventeenth-Century Europe (hereafter: *Origins*), edited by Oliver Impey and Arthur MacGregor and published by the Clarendon Press division of the Oxford University Press in 1985, includes over thirty detailed studies by specialists in all aspects of this field, as well as over one hundred figures. A sort of companion volume, *Tradescant's Rarities: Essays on the Foundation of the Ash-*

molean Museum, 1683, with a Catalogue of the Surviving Early Collections (hereafter: *Tradescant's*), edited by Mr. MacGregor, was actually published two years earlier, in 1983, on the occasion of the museum's tercentenary, and includes almost two hundred plates. The Bacon citation derives from p. 1 of the *Origins* book. The Cope material is drawn from pp. 17ff. of *Tradescant's*.

(Also of interest in this context is the massive yet exquisitely turned catalogue to the 1991 "Age of the Marvelous" show at the Hood Museum of Art, Dartmouth College, New Hampshire [distributed by the University of Chicago Press]; the introductory essay, by the volume's editor, Joy Kenseth, includes sections on Novelty and Rarity, the Foreign and the Exotic, the Strange and the Bizarre, the Unusually Large and the Unusually Small, the Transcendent and the Sublime, the Surprising and the Unexpected . . . and the Waning of the Marvelous [which Kenseth dates at about 1700]. One might also want to look at the catalogue to the Danish National Museum's 1993 "Museum Europa: An Exhibition about the European Museum from the Renaissance to Our Time," with its chapters on "The Curious Eye," "The Reflecting Eye," "The Panoramic Eye," and "The Surreal Eye." Richard Ross's book of photographs *Museology*, published by Aperture in 1989, with an essay by David Mellor, is similarly compelling.)

Stephen Greenblatt's *Marvelous Possessions: The Wonder of the New World* was published by the University of Chicago Press in 1991. The material on wonder as the quintessential European response to the discovery of the New World and on the startle reflex is drawn from pp. 14–16. The Léry, Albertus Magnus, and de Certeau material is drawn from pp. 16–19. (Janet Whatley's translation of Jean de Léry's *History of a Voyage to the Land of Brazil, Otherwise Called America* was published by the University of California Press in 1990.) The discussion of the new credibility of the previously unbelievable in Léry, Díaz, and Raleigh also draws on Greenblatt (pp. 21–22, 163).

Adalgisa Lugli's essay "Inquiry as Collection" in the autumn 1986 issue of *Res* focuses, as its subtitle implies, on "The Athanasius Kircher Museum in Rome." Lugli's riff on "the problem of continuity" comes from p. 116. MacGregor on Rudolf II of Prague is from *Tradescant's* (p. 74).

The photographer and latter-day cabinetperson Rosamond Purcell curated a marvelous show at the temporary quarters of the Getty Center in Santa Monica, California, at the end of 1994, entitled "Special Cases: Natural Anomalies and Historical Monsters." The description of the Leiden cabinet ordered by type of defect comes from that show (as, incidentally, does the quotation from Edward Brown's 1673 *Brief Account of Some Travels in divers Parts of Europe* in the note on pp. 116–17 of this book). The pelican in Imperato's collection is explicated in Giuseppe Olmi's essay in *Origins* (p. 10), as well as in MacGregor's essay in the same volume (p. 148), although Purcell herself passionately demurs, insisting that the bird in question is in fact a spoonbill and not a pelican (everyone else's clever explications notwithstanding).

The moralizing skeletons at the Theatrum Anatomicum in Leiden were detailed in MacGregor's essay on

"Collectors and Collections of Rarities in the Sixteenth and Seventeenth Centuries" in *Tradescant's* (p. 78). Dr. Antonie Luyendijk-Elshout's account of Frederik Ruysch's *vanitas mundi,* drawn from her article "Death Enlightened" in the April 6, 1970, issue of the *Journal of the American Medical Association,* was cited in Th. H. Lunsingh Scheurleer's essay in *Origins* (p. 119). Rosamond Purcell and Stephen Jay Gould also relied heavily on Luyendijk-Elshout in the absorbing account "Dutch Treat: Peter the Great and Frederik Ruysch" in their spectacularly illustrated *Finders, Keepers: Treasures and Oddities of Natural History* (the account was enriched, as well, by a good deal of groundbreaking research by Ms. Purcell herself), and I, in turn, relied heavily upon them in my discussion of Ruysch (as well as upon Robert Massie's *Peter the Great: His Life and World* [New York: Knopf, 1980] and Simon Schama's *The Embarrassment of Riches* [New York: Knopf, 1987], and, regarding Rachel Ruysch, Germaine Greer's *The Obstacle Race* [New York: Farrar Straus, 1979]).

Descartes's misgivings about the *Wunderkammer* sensibility are aired in Greenblatt (pp. 19–20) and amplified upon (along with similar misgivings by other contemporaries) in William Schupbach's piece in *Origins* (pp.177–78). Lugli's discussion of Della Porta *et al.'s* position on wonder is from p. 123 of the *Res* article; James Gleick's delineation of Richard Feynman's position on doubt comes from his introduction to the 1994 Modern Library edition of Feynman's 1965 *The Character of Physical Law* (pp. ix–x).

The history of the Tradescants and Elias Ashmole is

drawn from *Tradescant's*. The legal tangle regarding the bequest, for example, is covered on pp. 41–43 (with Hester's pond drowning on p. 43); the visit to the witchcraft trial is from p. 14; the travels of the elder Tradescant to Muscovy and the younger to Virginie are found on pp. 18 and 13, respectively; Tradescant the Elder's letter to the Secretary of the Navy is from pp. 19–20; the Stirn letter describing the collection and the "daintily" carved crucifixion is from pp. 20–21; the discussion of the Siege of Pavia, with map, is from pp. 318–26; and the catalogue entries on the fruit-stone carvings are from pp. 245–46. (Additional details were drawn from pp. 149–52 of *Origins*.)

The origin of the name "California" in the Amazon warrior passages of Rodríguez Montalvo's 1510 *Esplandián* novel is from Walter Bean's *California: An Interpretive History* (New York: McGraw-Hill, 1968; pp. 16–17), as are the details on Cabrillo's and Drake's California travels (pp. 17–20). For more on Cabrillo, see Maud Hart Lovelace's *What Cabrillo Found* (New York: Crowell, 1958). Drake in the Tradescant collection is from *Tradescant's* (pp. 93 and 314).

A monograph *Tell the Bees . . .: Belief, Knowledge and Hypersymbolic Cognition* is forthcoming, by way of the Society in conjunction with the Visitors, and should soon be available from the Museum of Jurassic Technology.

The Mütter Museum does exist and is quite wonderful. It can be found at the College of Physicians of Philadelphia (19 South Twenty-second Street, Philadelphia, PA 19103). Its 1994 traveling exhibit at the Museum of Jurassic Technology was curated by Laura

Lindgren, who also coordinates the Mütter's perennially mesmerizing annual calendar. One of the best accounts of the Mütter's history can be found in its director Gretchen Worden's entry, "Pathological Treasures of the Mütter Museum," in the *Encyclopaedia Britannica*'s 1994 Medical and Health Annual (pp. 76–79).

Incidentally: that "1579 Lupton" reference regarding the "flayne Mouse" cure: I couldn't help myself (you *knew* I wouldn't be able to)—I did end up having to pursue the matter, and the reference, naturally, is actual. Details can be found in *A Dictionary of Superstition*, edited by Iona Opie and Moira Tatem for the Oxford University Press (1989, p. 267) where the full title of Thomas Lupton's book is given as *A Thousand Notable Things of Sundry Sortes* (1579, with an enlarged edition, presumably not by Mr. Lupton himself, in 1660). Opie and Tatem also record the 1984 testimony of "a seventy-year-old man" to the effect that "When I was young, in Lincolnshire, when children used to wet their beds, their parents gave them roast mouse, fur and all, on toast to eat, and that stopped the bed-wetting" (p. 268).

I resolved not to delve any further into the stuff about urine and grandmothers.

Illustration Credits

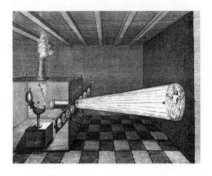

The Magic Lantern at Athanasius Kircher's museum, Rome (1678)

The author and publishers would like to begin by expressing their particular gratitude to the Society for the Diffusion of Useful Information, in Los Angeles, California, under whose generous auspices the plurality of images in this book appear (which is to say, all of those not otherwise credited). In addition the author and publishers gratefully acknowledge:

Front endpaper   Ole Worm's Museum, frontispiece to *Museum Wormianum*, 1655, courtesy of the Getty Research Center, Resources Collection, Santa Monica, California

Frontispiece   Charles Willson Peale, *The Artist in His Museum*, 1822, courtesy of the Pennsylvania Academy of the Arts, Philadelphia; gift of Mrs. Sarah Harrison (the Joseph Harrison, Jr. Collection)

Pp. 10–11 & 17   Drawings by Richard Hoyen, based on photos by Robin Palanker

P. 48   Stills from *Stasis*, courtesy of David Wilson

P. 57   Drawing of Sandaldjian Pope by Jesse Cantley

P. 59   Courtesy Lucas Nova Sensor, Fremont, California

Facing p. 68   Photo by and courtesy of Tom and Maria Eisner

P. 71   Photo by Heather Stone, courtesy of the *Knoxville News-Sentinel*

P. 78   Engraving by Theodor de Bry from his *Amerika*, Vol. II, pl. 35 (Frankfurt, 1590), courtesy of the Rare Books and Manuscripts Division, The New York Public Library, Astor, Lenox and Tilden Foundations

P. 82   Francesco Calceolari's museum, from the frontispiece of B. Ceruti and A. Chiocco, *Musaeum Francisci Calceolari Veronensis* (Verona, 1622), courtesy of the Getty Center

P. 85   Engraving of Theatrum Anatomicum in Leiden, after Jan Cornelisz van't Woudt (1610), courtesy of the Rijksmuseum, Amsterdam

P. 86   Engraving of Ruysch's *vanitas mundi* by C. Huyberts, from Ruysch's *Opera Omnia*, courtesy of the Getty Center

Pp. 92 & 97   Paintings of John Tradescant the Elder (attributed to Cornelis de Neve), John Tradescant the Younger and his wife Hester (attributed to Emanuel de Critz, 1656), and Elias Ashmole (by John Riley,

1689); and photographs of fruit-stone carvings: all courtesy of the Ashmolean Museum, Oxford University, England

Pp. 56, 105–6   Photos by Susan Einstein, courtesy of the Society for the Diffusion of Useful Information

Pp. 107–9   Photos by Rick Echelmeyer, courtesy of the Mütter Museum at the College of Physicians of Philadelphia

P. 111   Photo of David Wilson (the director outside his museum), photographer unknown, courtesy of the Society for the Diffusion of Useful Information

P. 115   Photo of Jorge Luis Borges by Charles Phillips, courtesy of Time Incorporated

P. 120   Engraving of Columbus in Cuba, by Bertolozzi after West, Bettmann Archive

P. 123   *The Anatomy Lesson of Dr. Frederik Ruysch* by Jan van Neck (1683), courtesy of the Amsterdam Historical Museum

P. 129   Engraving of Isaac Newton by Loudan, Bettmann Archive

P. 132   Engraving of Ole Worm from *Museum Wormianum* (1655), courtesy of the Getty Center

P. 141   Engraving of Mary Davis of Saughall from Ormerund's *History of the County Palatine and the City of Chester* (1676), courtesy of the Ashmolean Museum, Oxford

P. 149   Photo of satyr with cactus horns, courtesy of Tessa Rapaczynski

P. 160   Engraving of the Magic Lantern at Athanasius Kircher's museum in Rome, from *Museum Italieum*, vol. 71, courtesy of the Print Collection, Miriam and Ira D. Wallach Division of Art, Prints and

Photographs, The New York Public Library, Astor, Lenox and Tilden Foundations

Back endpaper   Ferrante Imperato's museum in Naples, Italy, from Imperato's *Dell'Historia Naturale di Ferrante Imperato Napolitano* (1599), courtesy of the Ashmolean Museum, Oxford

About the Author

LAWRENCE WESCHLER has been a staff writer for *The New Yorker* since the early 1980s, shuttling between political tragedies and cultural comedies, and is a two-time winner of the George Polk Award (for Cultural Reporting in 1989 and Magazine Reporting in 1992). His previous books include *Seeing Is Forgetting the Name of the Thing One Sees; The Passion of Poland; David Hockney's Cameraworks; Shapinsky's Karma, Boggs's Bills and Other True-Life Tales;* and *A Miracle, a Universe.* He lives in Westchester County, New York, with his wife and daughter.